Don't Leave *Your* Money Behind

How Expats can escape the trap of debt and financial stagnation

*by **Moses Chavi** FCCA, CIA, CFE, CRMA, CM*

There are many traps that have ruined and continue to ruin wonderful plans for many expats. With all the pomp and joy attached to the opportunity of getting an overseas job or contract, ill-executed transitions have ended many hopes in misery and regrets.

But there is a better way.
#don'tleaveyourmoneybehind

Don't Leave Your Money Behind

Skillsway Books

Email: mw@skillsway.org

bookmight
by skillsway

www.bookmight.com
www.skillsway.org

"Having spent 20 of the past 30 years in the Middle East as a professional services advisor, I have seen firsthand many of the challenges that Moses addresses in his book. I wish there had been such a well thought out guide for me to draw on in those early difficult days as a new expatriate. Moses has applied himself to developing this tool in the same way as he did when we worked together many years ago, it is a credit to him and the people he seeks to help."

Robert O'Hanlon - Partner at Deloitte

"The book "Don't Leave Your Money Behind" by Moses Chavi, reflects a conversational read that makes the financial content extremely palatable and anticipative. The author, a financial guru par excellence, penned his verbal financial advice expertly."

Dr. Johlene Ntwane PhD, MBA

"Well-articulated and wise advice for your financial independence, full of powerful and practical ideas, this most impactful book will change the way you think. It is a paradigm shift. Moses Chavi's authenticity, professionalism, and superb writing will make this book an incredible resource for helping you put your big dreams into action.

Moses Chavi has written an inspiring must-read book for everyone. Read it and learn from the best."

Adnan Suleiman - Strategic Finance and Audit professional, Governance, Risk and Compliance Consultant, Anti-Fraud & Corruption Expert

It is not only money that you need; it is the right attitude towards money that will reward your efforts as an expatriate. Your relationship to money is what needs to be re-aligned and transformed. Without that you may come out of the season of being an expatriate with nothing to show and a heart that is dissatisfied with the years of your effort. Build right and listen to the advice on the pages of this book by my dearest friend, Moses Chavi.

Motsamai Johannes Pule – Father & Husband, Marketing Professional

"The author delivers interesting insights concerning strategic management of personal finances. This book is a useful resource for meeting financial need in a resource constrained post-Covid environment. This invaluable book addresses practical insights and strategies for expats to avoid common mistakes.

A very important, useful, and timely contribution from Moses Chavi."

Dr. Tarek Rana PhD, MBA, CA, ACMA - Senior Lecturer in Accounting, School of Accounting, Information Systems and Supply Chain, RMIT University

Author Moses Chavi has penned his insights on personal finance management of expatriates by showing a clear path to navigate the challenges and pitfalls for handling money with greater efficiency and effectiveness. The Author highlights the psychological behaviour of the average human mind, covering how impulse and rational thinking impacts one's financial destiny. Moses has further gone deep into the subject with lot of research in multiple dimensions to hand hold an expat in protecting their hard-earned wealth with real life examples. He has also embedded spiritual aspects into human behavior on money matters with strong quotes and anecdotes from leading authors to support the arguments.

Wonderful book and a must read for all expats. The book is nicely written in a lucid language, with a lot of wisdom in fiscal discipline, planning, spending habits and negative effects of fantasy. A handbook to be read slowly over a period to digest its contents. The readers will gain a lot of knowledge in understanding the successful road map to wealth management for the long term.

Sampath Balaji - Managing Director and CXO Partner at CXO Prime LLC

"Imagine a soldier walking in the dark, blindfolded. Although holding his powerful gun, he is still most likely to be defeated by the enemy because he cannot see the enemy coming. Without the appropriate knowledge and discipline of making, growing, and keeping money, you are like the soldier walking in the dark. We all need a financial plan for our income in order to attain the unique visions of our lives. Planning lights up the way to the attainment of our goals. Without an appropriate financial plan, we are planning for a doomed financial future. Let us all learn from ants – in the season of plenty, they save for the future. Moses Chavi has written a book that shows expats how to avoid the pitfalls that can cause you to lose your hard-earned money; but most importantly, he

provides an easy-to-understand way on how to save and keep your earnings."

Armstrong Nhlabatsi PhD, Post-Doctoral Researcher (Cloud Security Modeling and Risk Assessment)

"Every dream is valid; and for those who have aspired to live and work abroad, the realization that they are actually living and working outside their country is a dream come true in itself. Life outside one's country can be fast, glittery, and happening; however, in all that, as a foreign national you may be floating in the moment, living the dream, and not paying as much attention to the money you are making - same money you crossed the oceans for - to earn and build a dream life back home. Planning one's money to build a nest is not something that just happens, it requires deliberate and intentional actions, to escape the trap that many expats fall into. This book "Don't Leave Your Money Behind: How Expats can escape the trap of debt and financial stagnation" highlights the core fundamentals of growing your wealth while living abroad without living less of your dreams in both worlds".

Bertha Mkandawire Munthali- International Researcher

DEDICATION

To Tusekile, Warren and Jessica. Beyond everything in this world, I admire your affection and gentleness.

TABLE OF CONTENTS

APPRECIATION

I thank God for the wisdom, the gifts, the support systems, and the ability to bring this book to life.

I would like to express my heartfelt gratitude to my dear wife Tusekile, and my lovely kids Warren and Jessica, who encouraged me through the 'mostly lonely' season of writing, coupled with extended moments of distracted attention.

Many thanks also to my dear friends and a global expat community that has walked this exciting international journey with me, and to those who participated in the expat survey which bolstered some of my thoughts and learnings documented in this book.

I am also indebted to my editorial team who were relentless to see this book published; and to my mentors, some of whom provided recommendations for this book.

PRAISE FOR THE AUTHOR

My wife and I met Moses Chavi and his wife a decade ago when he and I were both expatriates on the island nation of Bahrain. He was a young high-potential auditor, and I identified him as the type of person with whom I wanted to network, personally and careerwise.

This colleague-friendship has continued through the years, and he has reached the potential that I initially saw in him. What impresses the most about him is the balance in his life - advancing rapidly in his career, exhibiting leadership in his industry and community, having a close relationship with the wonderful family he is raising and pushing his quest to build a strong financial position - all on a sound spiritual foundation.

Therefore, Moses did not surprise me at all when he told me that he was writing a book about how to become a successful expatriate, and how to thrive so as not to allow the many trappings that get in the way of financial gain.

Yes, I've been there, done that and saw many of my colleagues lose their focus, spending their money on fancy designer clothes and purses, lavish exotic vacations and having the car or motorcycle which they had always dreamed of. They retired or left overseas life with way less to speak for it than they had hoped. "I was making so much money, why am I not leaving with solid savings?"

Expatriates everywhere will appreciate Moses sharing his experience and wisdom in his new book! I encourage those who read my 'praise note' to read this entire book, thoughtfully - if applicable, with their significant other - and, if they are spiritual, with prayerful consideration. Read on and be a better person and a better family! My greatest wish for all readers of this book is to become winners, financially. You will find Moses Chavi to be a great role model, starting with modest means and charting a path to multi-dimensional expatriate success!

Lawrence Martin Capuder - Cybersecurity Advisor – Florida, USA. Saudi Aramco Retiree.

PREFACE

This book is partly a memoir and a compilation of an expat's symphony of travel, adventure, hopes, experiences, grandeur, lessons, and realities of a global career. As a long-time sojourner myself, I have lived through the ups and downs of working in a foreign land plus the complexities of leading a beautiful family away from the place we call home.

For those of you who have lived the expat life before, or are doing so now, our experiences would resonate, and somehow, somewhere deep within us, there is a longing to be significant and to build ever-lasting wealth for ourselves, our children, and the entire posterity. We dream of generational wealth that would end the string of historical financial family struggles. If we were all financially sorted, international ventures would only be characterized by consultancy projects, trading, conferences, tourism, and lots of fun! Not working on a '9 to 5' job.

Beyond a blossoming career there is always a fundamental rationale why we desire to grab that international stint. For me it was to make some handsome cash – and then build my own consultancy firm back home after a well-planned 3-year period. After 12 years of working in multiple Gulf Countries, I have understood that the reality of 'getting stuck' in the diaspora is not a mere cliché. Many lives are spent and exhausted away from home for decades, but it still feels like it has only been yesterday when you first left home.

What about you? What was your reason for making the international move?

Every time I ask random expats this question it just appears as if almost everyone has lost their original 'why', and their current disposition is more of a mutated form of rationalization. Most of them would say they took the overseas role to make some good money over a targeted period of five years, on average - only to realize they have been outside their country for 20 years or more! And what about the money? (Laughs, cymbals, and trumpets!) Nothing. Most of them have nothing much to show for the massive expat contributions to the foreign lands.

To be fair with ourselves, we must live and survive, right? The monthly paychecks quickly run from the bank into the pockets, but only to be quickly whisked away by the same banks, soft creditors and all the demands of a fast life. Some of the interviewed expats lamented costly housing and school fees that mercilessly deplete the bank accounts before you even practice the left-right-left side mantra for crossing the road. Anyway, this could make a beautiful story for another day. But I am very sure you have been there before.

Mama said, "Embrace wisdom, and life will treat you well." As I get older, those words ring a validation bell. I wish I had learned earlier the lessons I only appreciated after falling into a ditch of debt and unheard financial burdens. I am one of the most qualified expats to write on this subject because I have made most of the mistakes that people like me make when they grab their first international move. I have done it all. Although I may sound like I enjoyed the experience, I genuinely appreciate the lessons learnt on this knotty journey. It has not been easy, but it has been massively helpful for my future and posterity. Every moment of mistakes and triumphs has been worth it.

In this book I bring you some of the deep lessons on living wisely in a foreign land; how to make a good buck and how to keep it. Not just how to save money, but also how to purposefully keep, grow and protect your money.

Although I have every right to brag and focus on my professional profile as an Accountancy Fellow and an international risk and internal audit consultant, this book is not about that type of corporate stuff. I will do the subject great injustice if I complicate our discussions in any way. This book is all about a heart-to-heart conversation; sharing the lessons learnt on this journey so that those who choose to gain wisdom will avoid the traps of a flashy and cozy life submerged in debt and with a far-fetched assurance of survival and financial breakthroughs.

The idea to write this book came at a time when innumerable expats suffered a heavy blow of losing jobs due to the global Covid19 pandemic which engulfed the surface of the earth since November 2019. Visibly, many industries have been heavily affected to the point of being left with no option but to retrench their staff with the hope of saving a shaky bottom line. Although citizens of the heavily affected nations also suffered pretty much a similar fate, the heavy effects were and have been felt by the expat communities.

It saddened my heart to see how families were torn apart at the news of losing the 'only source' of income' amidst the obligations to pay back massive loans solicited in the 'days of plenty,' when the markets were liquid. And then there were many expats who worked in countries that do not release retrenched residents who have debt in their financial systems. This episode meant the non-working spouses and kids returned home leaving the bread winner in the foreign land until they could figure out life. It is a sad but practical situation.

Being someone who has been on the debt side of life for the longest period, I understand the pain, the fears, the shame, and the embarrassment of having to ask friends and family to bail you out of a situation you did not foresee.

The biggest pain of debt is that by the time you get to the point of paying back, oftentimes you cannot even remember what you used the borrowed money for. If you bought a car, you would be lucky to still see it in your driveway; nonetheless, it is not that mint shiny thing anymore. It has become just one of the mobility apparatuses that does not excite you anymore. If you borrowed funds for a 'brilliant project', you may find yourself at a time when the project has flopped, and you do not even know where it all went. And if you borrowed for food, furniture, entertainment, and even school fees, the passage of time makes every penny you spent unjustifiable and non-traceable. This is called 'life simply happening 101'.

This book is about the genesis. The 'why' of the international episode. We need to go back to the core purpose of our expat journeys and how we can configure the entire episode around financial wisdom to ensure we do not leave our money behind.

This book is indeed about financial freedom. I wish I could have the mental space and ability to write on how to coin a successful overseas career - but my mission, truly, is financial freedom. The burden upon my heart is how wonderful people can enjoy overseas careers without falling into the debt-and-fake-life trap, and how they can return home wealthier and happier than they left. This is important for all of us.

Although this book has a focused mission for global expats, the wisdom within its pages is applicable to anybody: including couples, single parents, singles, professionals, artisans, business owners, and any person who is tired of the status quo and broken dreams. Anyone who is seeking lasting financial independence and freedom. The wisdom of the ages resonates across all facets of life and is never limited to the privileged few. Wisdom is never monopolized.

Having no financial plan is the surest way to fail. It takes grit and a solid financial mindset to grow your savings and build generational wealth.

#don’tleaveyourmoneybehind

Purpose & Financial Vision

"Redirecting your compass towards meaningful success"

1

CHAPTER 1: Your Purpose, Personal Vision and Money

We all desire wealth; whether born in opulence or poverty, there is a place at the center of the human psyche that holds ambitions and propels us towards personal achievement. This understanding resonates with every expat who leaves the comfort of their homeland to pursue a worthwhile adventure in a foreign land, with a greater percentage targeting money. Even for someone who may argue that money is not everything, at least we can agree that money fuels comfort, safety, progress, and ambitions. I recall an interesting conversation with a friend around this subject where he pondered: "do you know, Moses, that the people who usually say money is not everything are mostly the rich ones?" That's right. I echoed his revelation. "And do you know that until you've had your basics covered and your key ambitions achieved you would not make such statements?" I said, most likely. It is known that money may not protect you against adverse 'acts of God' but for sure it does answer a lot of life's pressing needs. The most beneficial act is to find its place within your purpose and personal vision.

"Life is one big road with lots of signs. So when you riding through the ruts, don't complicate your mind. Flee from hate, mischief, and jealousy. Don't bury your thoughts, put your vision to reality. Wake

Up and Live!" - Bob Marley

If you can't see your future, life loses its meaning, and it becomes very easy to get entangled in so many unhealthy 'busy-mess'. One enduring phrase says, *"without a vision the people perish,"* or they become clueless, without restraint, and with no focus. More particularly, personal vision is what keeps you busy during the day - and awake at night. You do not operate on a machine-gun basis. You have a clear tunnel vision; you surely must have one!

It is this personal vision that helps you define your purpose.

I know you may be wondering how the topic of vision and purpose made it into the first chapter of this financial book. These facets are everything. In fact, it will be futile to jump into financial freedom discourses without tackling these fundamentals.

A personal vision is the future you desire to attain after the completion of specific efforts; whilst purpose, describes 'why' you exist and the activities you need to complete before you exit the surface of the earth. In fact, the simple reminder that one day we will exit this earth should keep us busy searching for our purpose. Rarely is purpose dropped in our lap in a dream or a divine vision. It is in those daily menial activities that we get to find our purpose. In my modest number of years in this world I've realized that it is the people who keep on moving that somehow get to find their 'eureka moment' that ends up defining the depth of their existence.

We are all on this planet for a purpose. Even if you don't feel like it somedays, there is a deeper purpose why you are here, and it is your sole duty to discover it. Yes, sometimes God can reveal himself to you and push you towards his divine plans; but even if he does not, one day you will encounter the light of purpose pushing you into your destiny. The secret lies in your tenacity and focus – in that subtle spirit of never giving up. The world yearns for your gift.

"You are not here merely to make a living. You are here in order to enable the world to live more amply, with greater vision, with a finer spirit of hope and achievement. You are here to enrich the world, and you impoverish yourself if you forget the errand." - Woodrow Wilson

How is Your Money Tied to Purpose and Vision?

People who know why they are here, and where they are heading, always exhibit rare traits that define their inclination towards life and, subsequently, their bank account. This rare breed of people usually benefit from the following pillars of purpose and vision:

- They understand the adage of being in the right place at the right time.
- They choose their friends and connections wisely.
- They understand beneficial influences and who to listen to.
- They know the type of books to read, and the discipline required in this endeavor.
- They are not swayed by circumstances.
- They understand which paths not to take.
- They know which opportunities to accept and which ones to ignore entirely.
- They lead simplified lives.
- They spend money on things that add value and eternal wealth.
- They live peacefully with all men as much as it depends on them.

- They add value to everything that lands in their hands.
- People love them, and they enthuse sincere love towards others.
- They are contented and always filled with gratitude.
- They prize their time like professionals.
- They value family and friends.
- Their mindset is set on eternal and enduring things.
- They live large without breaking the bank.
- They have a rare type of discretion in matters of life.
- They are spontaneous but not fire-fighters.
- They are not surprised with life because they walk according to a solid plan.
- They value life and understand the benefits of taking care of their bodies, mind, and soul.
- They are avid learners, and they do not despise their teachers.
- They are intentional on the educational programs they adopt.

- They are not boastful.
- They are humble and not prideful.
- They are strong-willed but not negatively egoistic.
- They do that 'one thing' that brings supernatural breakthroughs in big areas of life.
- They know exactly how to react to both good news and tragedies.
- They are men and women of faith. They look up to God beyond their own wisdom.
- They are prayerful and do not run a display of mere religiosity.
- They are faithful to their partners.
- They honor and respect their parents and guardians.
- They understand value-for-money and the opportunity cost of everything they do.
- They understand the power in the answer 'no'.
- They surround themselves with people and programs that

inspire and excite their minds towards the revealed paths.

- They are trailblazers. They do not simply follow every old pattern.
- They create enduring value.
- Their contributions flow into the nations and future generations.

Your Purpose and Vision for the Expatriate Adventure

According to the 2020 World Migration Report by the United Nations International Organization for Migration (IOM), "a scale of international migration increase was observed in line with recent trends. At the end of 2019, the number of international migrants was estimated to be almost 272 million globally, with nearly two-thirds being labor migrants. This figure remains a very small percentage of the world's population (at 3.5%), meaning that most people globally (96.5%) are estimated to be residing in their country of origin.

However, the estimated number and proportion of international migrants already surpasses some projections made for the year 2050, which were in the order of 2.6% or 230 million. That said, it is widely recognized that the scale and pace of international migration is notoriously difficult to predict with precision because it is closely connected to acute events (such as severe instability, economic crisis or conflict) as well as long-term trends (such as demographic change, economic development, communications technology advances and transportation access)".

The 2020 report further drew insights from long-term data that international migration is not uniform across the world but is shaped by economic, geographic, demographic and other factors resulting in distinct migration patterns, like migration "corridors" developed over many years.

The 2020 World Migration Report indicated that India had the largest number of migrants living abroad (17.5 million), followed by Mexico and China (11.8 million and 10.7 million respectively). The top destination country remained the United States (50.7 million international migrants). Labor migration has contributed to significant population changes, especially in Gulf Cooperation Council (GCC) States. With the exceptions of Oman and Saudi Arabia, migrants made up the majority of the populations in GCC countries. As of 2023, the GCC consist of Saudi Arabia, the United Arab Emirates, Qatar, Bahrain, Kuwait, and Oman.

It is pertinent to acknowledge that the migrant numbers would be better understood if compartmentalized into workers *(both white collar and blue collar),* accompanying spouses and kids, students, refugees, asylum seekers, and others. There is always a provision for 'others' as we cannot really know how everyone gets to find themselves across the border.

Anyway, for those of us who are experienced expats, did we have a solid purpose and vision before we left home?

When you are planning a deliberate international move, you need to be clear about what you want to achieve by finding your why. There is need for a sober reflection on why you are leaving your local job or your business venture to get into an international placement - and where that would put your family, or your future plans.

It is not everyone who writes down their plan or thinks about their life in terms of what they want to achieve in personal growth, financial growth, career growth and other critical areas of life. There are a lot of life domains that we can articulate in this book about setting personal goals; but for the sake of this book, we will focus on the 'whys' that affect and influence an international move.

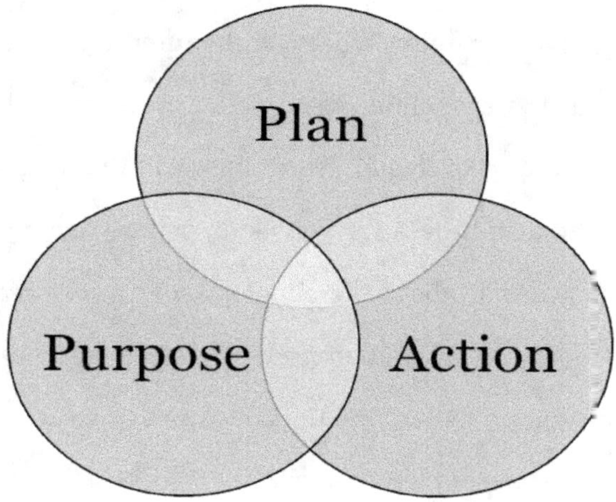

Whether you are squeezed in your current job, or you do not have an attainable growth agenda in the current environment, you can decide to go overseas because you have a specific target to bolster your professional career, or to gain unique experience from a targeted industry or country. But before you do that, there is a need to reflect what that overseas opportunity means to you - what it means for your family and your future. If you are currently getting a US$3,000 monthly paycheck back home, and the international move promises to pay you US$10,000 monthly, obviously that is a lucky jump. If you get triple pay with all the required benefits, in a normal sense, you will most likely decide to make an immediate move.

However, even after getting excited about the job offer, you still need to catch your breath, sit down and intelligently evaluate why you are really excited about that opportunity. What will the international move entail when you look at the economic index of the prospective destination? What is the known cost of living? How much will the housing cost be, what about the education fees for your kids or for your own personal development - and what about the simpler aspects *(not really simple when you get down to it)*, but important aspects such as finding a helper who can support you around the house and take care of your kids - especially if both spouses plan to work?

What about the possibility that accompanying spouses may not be allowed to get a job or do business in the overseas location? How would such realities affect your monthly income? These are questions that should be answered before you take the leap of faith.

"People pay for what they do, and still more for what they have allowed themselves to become. And they pay for it very simply; by the lives they lead." - James Baldwin

This book is about money - how you can surely make some, get some, and keep some in your expat journey. When I digress into other matters of life, simply understand that I am still thinking about the core message - how we can all make sure we don't lose a greater portion of our earnings in avoidable traps.

So, after considering the basics, what does that look like for you? If everything about the probable move still makes sense after reviewing your responses to the foregoing questions, then you need to plug in the numbers into your plans and get excited about how much you will be making! That means, by taking a calculated move, you can objectively complete your financial plan and vision.

In any case, if you have a specific financial goal, assuming the move is majorly about money, it is also important to get clear not just on the top line, or gross pay, but also estimate your expenditures as much as possible to somehow figure out your net pay - or what I would call the 'real take home pay' after tax *(if applicable)* and all major fixed costs such as housing, utilities, education, monthly groceries, home support, vehicle rentals and maintenance, and primary subscriptions, as applicable to your circumstances. This means that if you strictly spread your plan across the years, you can tell early-on that all you need to do is to essentially work on the international job for the next, say, 3 or 5 years and you can come back home financially sorted. Woohoo!

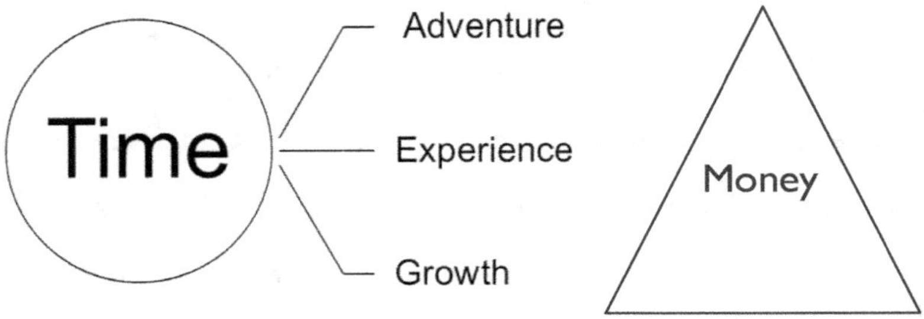

Devising a Money Plan

We started with the missionary questions tackling whether you know your vision and purpose before you define your rationale for taking the overseas opportunity. And this also brings us the question of whether you already know what you want to do with the money from the new opportunity. Do you already have an idea? Is it to start a business, open your own consulting firm, or to invest in the stock market, real estate, or head to the Bahamas? Can we assume that all these matters are clear for you at this stage?

Will the money that will be made over the committed period be enough to realize those dreams? If it is, then you can lock-in the time during which you will be disciplined enough until you go back to establish your business and fulfil the other ambitions. But if you do not have the basics, then what happens is that you go overseas with an indefinite target, and you realize that after 5, 10, 20 years or more, you get surprised that there is not much that has happened in your life apart from earning the salary, paying for your rent and school fees, making sure you survive and eat, helping people, and then you get old with time. You simply become an encyclopedia on the pitfalls of an expatriate life. You will agree that we cannot call that a purposeful or focused life. Unfortunately, time never waits for us – it keeps on ticking and clocking. Our duty is to harness time to our advantage.

It is essential to think-through your plan - even if your international agenda is only career growth, the pattern of thought and discipline will be the same. You need to know whether the international role will give you a clear personal advantage in terms of your personal development, the type of exposure in the targeted industry - what type of skills you will acquire, and the brand affiliation on your resume, among other benefits. How will the knowledge transfer benefit your future business or home country roles, especially if you plan to return home someday? It should be clear to you that if you bring that skill back home you will be valuable to the local economy.

If your international move is about full immigration for your family and the generations to come, meaning, you are not going back home *(forever and ever)* it is a completely different story that deserves a whole new book. But in part, I would say, that decision also requires a tangible plan. A heavy one for that matter. If you are thinking of moving out to the new country forever, the first thing I presume you would already know is whether that country provides permanent visas to foreigners or let alone their passport. Most countries do not easily give permanent residence to immigrants unless they make a solid investment in real estate and specific growth business sectors. It is important that you get clear on the possibility of you getting that destination's permanent residence visa and passport within approved means. It is crucial to be clean in matters of law. Protect your integrity at all costs.

A plan to immigrate is completely different from a mere move to get a job and make some bucks. Your research should be based on reliable sources and comprehensive assessment by people on the ground, especially friends and family, on how they managed to pull-off the immigration debacle, and what living under the roof of those countries looks like. Is it a matter of getting a prestigious passport, or is there an attached advantage that you are looking for? For example, do you want to start a business in that country, or do you want your children to have access to the best education system offered by that country? Are your kids, as your next generation, having the best access, and massive opportunities, beyond education (as citizens of their new home)? Are they going to be treated well? Does the culture expose them to what they need to be exposed to in terms of quality of life, faith and religion, family values, innovation, and personal growth? There are a lot of things that sum up life. All these things need to be thought through before you decide to migrate.

During the writing journey of this book, some family friends who had moved from the Arabian Gulf to a new country that easily offers permanent visas confided about their fears and concerns over the future of their kids after they realized that schoolteachers and some institutions had more authority over their kids' choices than them *(as biological parents).* These are some of the realities expats have to grapple with when making both temporary and permanent moves.

I appreciate that if your country is going through some tragic political chaos you do not really have an option, do you? But if you are coming from a peaceful and growing nation, you truly need to have a proper and sustainable reason for migration. Without much thought and research on your international move, you may end up being one human statistic that happily pushes the next generation into captivity and 'second class' environments, which is not worth the struggle and the opportunity cost. Your kids will take this against you. Of course, we all have personal priorities but candid advice from a legitimate source does not hurt.

For sure there are numerous stories of immigrant families that have achieved great things in foreign lands, including amassing millions of dollars through enterprise, or their kids going on to become star athletes representing their newly-found homes. This could be your dream too; and a noble one for that matter. All you need is a solid plan that resonates with your 'big dreams'.

"Desires dictate our priorities, priorities shape our choices, and choices determine our actions." - Dallin H. Oaks

Personal Financial Goals

Let us say you are guaranteed monthly savings of US$500, US$1,000, S$3,000, or more than US$5,000. You multiply this by 12 months, then by whatever number of years you plan to work overseas, say five years for example. After the five years, the US$3,000 monthly savings will translate to US$180,000, and the US$1,000 monthly earnings will produce US$60,000. Will this amount be enough to meet your financial goals (without complicating the figures with interest, inflation, or dividends)? If yes, then you need to set a disciplined target of this amount and pray for God's grace to allow you to realize this target. Life has wolves and many strange ways of stealing your hard-earned cash. A simple emergency can wipe out your hard-earned cash at the speed of light. That's why we all need divine covering in this subject of making and keeping money.

Do you see how tantalizing talking in numbers is? When you start projecting your earnings it gets even better. If you've never done the magic calculation of your targeted monthly savings *X* 12 months *X* the targeted number of expat years, just try it and raise the excitement of moving to the next step of developing your financial goals.

Writing Down Your Financial Goals

For companies, you will notice that they do not say 'our vision and purpose'. They usually say our vision and mission. For individuals, the mold fits better when we focus on our purpose and vision, which ultimately culminate into our earthly mission. To succeed in this mission, we need to set goals that will help us stay on course and indicate whether we are achieving the right targets.

It is pertinent to write down how we are going to move towards our vision, and how each stage of life will bolster our purpose. This is where goal-setting comes in. Corporate literature encourages us to create **SMART** goals, which implies that our goals must be **S**pecific,

Measurable, **A**ttainable, **R**elevant, and **T**ime-bound. A **specific** goal spells out what needs to be achieved, what work or resources will be required, and the articulate steps that will be taken to achieve the goal.

A **measurable** goal provides clear numbers, quantities, dates and specifics that can be utilized to 'measure' your progress towards the goal, and to ascertain whether you are winning or losing. An **achievable** goal does not stop you from dreaming audacious (or almost impossible) goals; this simply means you need to write down a goal that can be attained within the given time period. For example, if your bank account is overdrawn today, it will take more than a miracle to make you a millionaire within one year – but maybe a US$20,000 target within one year may be more achievable. A **relevant** goal should be tied to your personal vision, e.g., why do you want to achieve this particular goal, and how does that connect to your purpose or future plans? And finally, a **time-bound** goal will be tied to a specific timeline. Goals act like performance catalysts when tied to a specific date, just like what happens with academic examinations. Students engage in serious studies and exam preparations when they realize that the school will not shift the poles just to favor them. Same with our personal goals. It does not become a goal until it is attached to a specific date.

Example of a SMART goal.

I will raise and save **US$250,000** over the next **5 years**, by **31st December 2028**. This will be achieved through a disciplined expenditure approach whereby **US$50,000** will be set-aside **annually**, and my total **monthly expenses** will be limited to **US$5,000**; and I will create a **standing order** over my current bank account to ensure **automated** amounts go to a separate savings account. I will also create a **separate emergency account** targeting US$500 monthly contributions to ensure I do not get tempted to use the savings funds for any emergencies. To achieve this plan, I will **only travel for vacation every other second year** to avoid breaking the bank annually.

My spouse will be my **accountability partner** to ensure we **stay on this course** together. This 5-year financial target will help us achieve the required funds to **bootstrap our family investment**, and any **interest and dividends earned** on the invested cash (during the 5 years) will be a boost to the **investment goal**, or will be used to activate **another investment avenue**.

Mind you, life is exciting in the sense that the future does not merely flow towards us. Life will move on, whether we have goals or not; but it will not bring us the desired future. If you don't have a plan and accompanying goals, it is like giving permission to a stranger to run your life, and they will choose your house, food, clothes, location, education, car, and all necessities. What a life!

"By failing to prepare, you are preparing to fail." - Benjamin Franklin

If you are just starting your international career, you have the advantage of time to make good plans before you plunge into unnecessary chaos. It means you can have a different narrative than someone who is already *trapped* by the 'shiny life'. You can assess the opportunity deeply before you make some crucial decisions. But I also want to talk to experienced expats, those who have been *bruised* by life and perhaps still being bruised now.

Later, in Chapter 9, we will discuss in detail how we can successfully create a family financial plan.

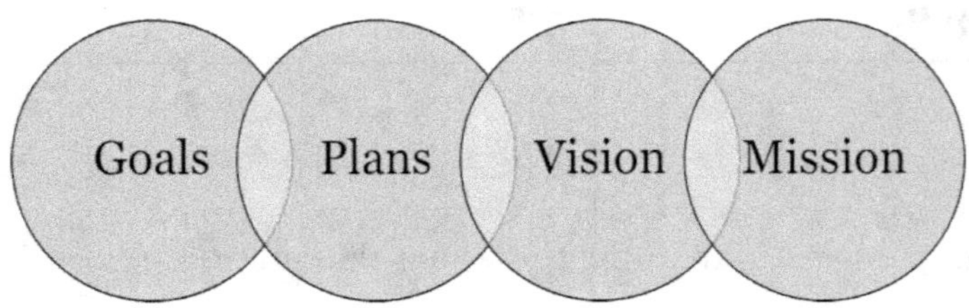

Without a clear vision, any quest for meaning becomes meaningless, and oftentimes, fruitless.

#don'tleaveyourmoneybehind

Intentionality

"The art of doing the right things for the right reasons"

2

Chapter 2: Be Intentional

You will realize that every chapter in this book is very connected to the core subject and all of them are tied to purpose. That is why purpose remains the most important chapter in the entire book.

The Art of Intentionality

What is it about being intentional? It is crucially important that as an individual you develop principles that define who you are, what you do, what you condone and what you don't; what you embrace and what you don't; plus, every value-driver that moves you to your intended life goals. This is important because in this age, we are bombarded every day by numerous options, and the direction we will take depends on the power of either your internal or external stimuli. If you are not intentional in what you do you will have a lot of people setting your life agenda on your behalf.

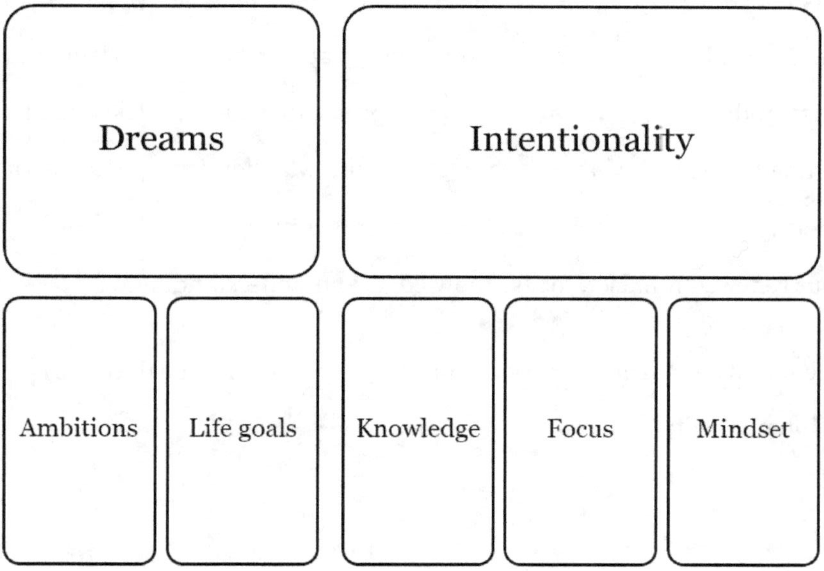

You will find people who will determine what you need to wear, eat, and which friends you need to hang out with, which car you need to drive, which part of town you need to live in; and you keep on being pulled around by the waves of other people's goals and intentions. That is why you need to be very careful that, after having defined your purpose, you become super selective on those you allow to speak to your senses.

Make sure to hold on to that clear mandate for your life, whether as a general-purpose or a specific one; what you see happening in your future, family, and the people involved in your life affairs, your society, and for your nation; the dreams you have and the goals you need to attain. Hold on to the defined strategies that will help you attain your most audacious goals. Anyone who speaks to your mind should be inclined towards what you are all about, whether in agreement or offering contrasting opinions. Your intentionality will be determined by your renewed mindset, focus, knowledge, and understanding.

The following passages carry the fundamentals of what I call the Art of Intentionality.

The Work of Choosing Friends

This crucial reflection on your dreams will take you back to say, if today you decide the type of friends you need to have, you are very intentional, knowing that these are the people who will help you to move towards that destination. But if you just choose friends on the basis of a simple stumbling into a place, and the people you meet look like good people, this is not sufficient rationale to propel you towards your intended goals and vision. You need to be careful how you choose friends. Get yourself people that you know will add value to your life. These are people who will equally open the door to their lives for you to serve them through generational wisdom and even economic impact. The adage goes, *iron sharpens iron*. You don't want to be the only iron among clay!

Of course, you don't self-aggrandize in the sense that all good things should only happen to you – or being selfish, nepotistic, and racialize the choosing of friends. Rather, you create a space whereby everyone who gets an opportunity to interact with you will be positively impacted for a lifetime. Although good things should happen to you (*and don't feel apologetic about it*), intentional friendships help create abundant and lasting value for all your connections. I strongly believe the world has enough success for everyone.

It is worthwhile to think about only good things, noble things, and excellent things; things that are praiseworthy, and things of good report. Anything that is virtuous should openly occupy our minds. To this effect, people with bad and negative vibes should not be tolerated in our circle. This matter may sound like a cliché but trust me, this issue is more spiritual than motivational. It is true that you will most likely turn out to be like some of your closest friends. Choose wisely.

If your friends are self-driven and possess default inspirational settings, your personal mission should be able to propel them towards their own intended purposes.

"Don't make friends who are comfortable to be with. Make friends who will force you to lever yourself up." — Thomas J. Watson

"Life is partly what we make it, and partly what it is made by the friends we choose." — Tennessee Williams

"Find a group of people who challenge and inspire you; spend a lot of time with them, and it will change your life." — Amy Poehler

"Do not be misled: Bad company corrupts good character." (1 Corinthians 15:33, NIV)

The Lifestyle Paradigm

What about your lifestyle? What type of a lifestyle do you lead and want? Would you be, for example, exposing your body to toxic stuff and substances? Alternatively, do you want to take care of your body? As much as we are talking about setting our financial goals, having a financial plan, and making money, all these do not make sense in an environment where your body is giving away. You may make all the money you want, but if you are not healthy, no financial success would truly bring you joy and fulfilment. It will not make sense if financial success finds you on the hospital bed. Or you may have consistent ailments that will not allow you to enjoy your money in peace. Or you may simply find your body sagging because of wrong food choices and because you hate sweating it out on the treadmill and doing some cardio exercises. Eventually, your sagginess will end up affecting your energy, the vitality that you need to build audacious goals or to build that global product or service that will inspire generations.

You cannot really inspire people if you yourself are not inspired. So, in terms of lifestyle, you need to choose the type of food to be eating and the type of physical exercises you will be doing and the frequency.

It does no harm to sometimes consider adopting a presidential diet. Being important citizens, most of these people must have healthy eating habits. But wisdom will direct you to stay away from the obvious chaos.

If you study the lives of successful and effective people, you will quickly realize that they have an intentional pattern of making sure they exercise their muscles every day. They eat proper foods, the kind of veggies and fruits most of us do not (really) like. In addition, they get the required amounts of healthy protein and carbohydrates. They don't aggrandize over a meal as if there isn't tomorrow.

You can tell by my credentials that I am neither a nutritionist nor a qualified health expert. But you cannot fake some of these fundamentals. If you eat like an elephant, you bet one day you will come out of that kitchen looking like one. I will not even try hard to breakdown the food portions that you need. Many people have tons of information on nutrition but only a handful would truly apply the lessons learnt to convert their knowledge into wisdom.

As well said by Jim Rohn, *"Success is nothing more than a few simple disciplines, practiced every day."*

Today, most of the streaming services have made everyone who has a pot, spoon, cooker, and smartphone, a nutrition expert. Check out the videos on YouTube. Numerous vloggers are talking about these things. You must listen to at least one of them. It may change your life.

Be intentional about this because intentionality will help you screen even the very food that gets through your mouth. You will start to question why you sleep 12 hours a day when your body is able to survive and cope well with 7 hours of rest, and even less on goal-getting days. Being intentional means wisely determining how much time you need to sleep. The wise man, Solomon, once said "*A little sleep, a little slumber, a little folding of the hands to rest, and poverty will come on you like a thief and scarcity like an armed man".*

What About the Books You Are Reading and The Stuff You Are Watching?

Intentional life will direct you to the right kind of books you read and the stuff you watch on TV or streaming services. If you are clear on what you need from this life, it becomes easy to know which books contain the kind of stuff that will lead you to 'the land of Canaan'. You cannot be binging on fiction and fantasies like a pro whilst purposefully neglecting the fundamental lessons such as service to others, leadership, success, entrepreneurship, spirituality and personal development.

The fact that you are reading this book right now is evidence enough that you are driven to change your life. You do not want to live a mediocre life. If you have already gone beyond the barriers of financial and personal stagnation, maybe you are reading to add value to other people's lives and to improve what you are already doing right now.

Your choice on the kind of books you read is driven by intentional living, hence you purposefully read value-adding books because they drive you towards your dreams. Within your continuous learning agenda, you need to identify areas that deserve a higher dose of knowledge, including financial management and investment books. Don't get on the simpletons' bandwagon of reading just any other book for the sake of being seen that you read books. Instead, choose books that resonate with the areas you are trying to 'sharpen your axe in'. If your problem is finances, you make sure you invest in finance books. The same applies to personal fitness, weight-loss, career growth and leadership.. Further, whatever you are learning, make sure you do not fall into the deception of merely getting entertained by reading books, and being known for posting on Facebook the numbers of completed books, and not necessarily how such books are transforming your life. If you do not do what the books say, then you are deceiving yourself and wasting your time as the world continues to progress.

The meaning of wisdom is the application of the knowledge that we gain from various sources, including books. Go beyond the excitement of merely reading books; otherwise come next year you will be surprised that you are stuck in the same position, probably with a bigger library and a ton of bank loans!

I don't need to be a prophet to predict that if you choose not to do anything about your current situation you will be in the same place next year. Even if you choose to let time heal the chaos, including paying off your loans (thinking that you need to chill and time will see the debt ebb away), it does not work that way. The reality is that if you do not change the habits that brought you here you will end up chasing the same shadows and even get into more debt. If everything is left to chance, next year you may not even be in the same position, but rather, in a worst position.

Whatever books you are reading to take you out of your unique situation, make sure you apply what you are learning, and it must be proven (through verifiable traits and behaviour) that you are taking different action plans to those that messed up your past years. This is particularly important. I cannot stress this enough.

Personal Development

By this day and age, we all should understand that life moves in growth-phases. If we do not grow our capacity in the comprehension of life itself, our persona, career, and investments – don't get it twisted – life will continue to progress, and we will continue to age. This is a guarantee of life. Our environment will continue to be redefined by new factors of development.

Either you will be faced with more learned, versatile, and fresh people coming into your workplace, or, for business people, you will constantly be bombarded by new start-ups and digital enterprises that will try to usurp your grip on the existing customer base. This is called life on the move, or as I call it, "Life is Happening" "LIH".

If you are a teacher or someone in the education business, it needs no prophecy to see that this domain is disrupted, and continues to be disrupted, by the numerous online learning solutions, artificial intelligence (AI), plus many creative minds that are having quantum leaps in everything they choose to invent or innovate. If you are sleeping and stuck, you are guaranteed never to catch up with these minds; or else choose now to change the trajectory of your business or career, or pretty much just close shop and completely start something new, maybe goat farming.

It is crucial to get intentional about your personal development. Your value system needs to ever evolve, and you need to get more knowledge or qualifications as long as everything you attain drives you towards the intended goals, and to ensure you remain relevant and competitive in the marketplace.

"Fools fold their hands and ruin themselves".

"Diligent hands will rule, but laziness ends in forced labor".

- King Solomon

I have seen many older folks, meaning those aged over 50 years, who have mastered computers and enterprise applications, and who can do far much better system optimizations and efficient work collaborations than many younger folks. I have also seen another cohort within the same age range who believe they can only lead and let all the crunchy stuff be done by the younger generation. However, there is an evil that lingers within the workplace and keeps on trolling such stagnant folks to their own demise. If the company is spending a triple package for your massive experience, be sure that the younger guys will easily feed from your massive experience just for a little while, then triple their impact through technology, and easily do the same things you have done for the past 30 years (and even much better) at a miniscule percentage of your salary.

For a capitalist environment, your services would no longer be justifiable at the current cost, and unfortunately you may never see those corridors of power again. So be careful what you wish for. If you still have the capacity and tenacity to read some books and engage in some form of digital training, gather yourself and do that. As an example, for business managers, marketers, accountants, auditors, engineers, project managers, and other relevant roles, data science has become more of a norm than that rare old qualification. Most businesses will soon expect to see data science or 'its siblings' on your resume.

For entrepreneurs and business owners, today it does not take a miracle to disrupt the market and push you out of the envied position. For some sectors, it is as simple as optimizing a social media marketing strategy and creating some awesome online pages! For some, it takes re-inventing or reverse engineering your products and services to produce a formidable competition just across the state, road, or block. And with the growing globalization (I do not think it is 'growing' away), you need to keep on chasing customers and trying to convince them that your local product or service is better and affordable than the one online.

This business space needs more brains, sleepless nights, excellent teams and an ever-evolving business and marketing strategy. You cannot afford to sleep like a king when your business demands a servant hand to pull it out of the mediocre market position. You also need to continue grabbing insights from similar businesses around the globe and see how experts are generating more promoter scores (customer likings and commendations) in other geographic locations, and how their approach resonates with your business back home.

"Don't wish it was easier, wish you were better. Don't wish for less problems, wish for more skills. Don't wish for less challenge, wish for more wisdom." – Jim Rohn

When you consistently place yourself in a position of open-learning, you then start to evolve into a thought-leader, and people start to seek your services and insights because you would have become more valuable. You cannot give people what you do not have. Even for a normal trading business, people require your advice above and beyond the product that you are selling. In a workplace, your colleagues or interacting units depend on you to add your 'brains' and thoughts to the services you are providing within the company. You cannot just type some stuff, present and then close shop. No. Life's ecosystems do not function that way.

Personal development is sealed by reading, classroom or online learning, travelling, meeting new people, getting on some adventure with strangers, family outings, getting new certifications enrolling into a bachelors or master's program, gaining some formal or informal leadership certificates, attending seminars or workshops, embarking on a new career all-together, starting a side business, getting into an investment partnership, or simply deciding to start investing in listed company stocks – plus whatever you decide to do that is different from what you have been doing in the past years. Just make sure you are not idle.

I challenge you to do more. That is the only way to create lasting value. We need to be intentional about personal development, because if you are stuck in one place, it becomes so difficult to attract the opportunities that will cause you to earn more money. You need to intentionally grow and attract value. Become something different and be ready to accommodate more success.

There is an ancient parable taught on how to manage your talents. It talks about a master who left some talents or tokens to his three servants before he embarked on a long journey. Check out the sobering excerpt below!

"For it will be like a man going on a journey, who called his servants and entrusted to them his property. To one he gave five talents, to another two, to another one, to each according to his ability. Then he went away. He who had received the five talents went at once and traded with them, and he made five talents more. So also he who had the two talents made two talents more. But he who had received the one talent went and dug in the ground and hid his master's money.

Now after a long time the master of those servants came and settled accounts with them. And he who had received the five talents came forward, bringing five talents more, saying, 'Master, you delivered to me five talents; here, I have made five talents more.' His master said to him, 'Well done, good and faithful servant. You have been faithful over a little; I will set you over much. Enter into the joy of your master.' And he also who had the two talents came forward, saying, 'Master, you delivered to me two talents; here, I have made two talents more.' His master said to him, 'Well done, good and faithful servant. You have been faithful over a little; I will set you over much. Enter into the joy of your master.'

He also who had received the one talent came forward, saying, 'Master, I knew you to be a hard man, reaping where you did not sow, and gathering where you scattered no seed, so I was afraid, and I went and hid your talent in the ground. Here, you have what is yours.' But his master answered him, 'You wicked and slothful servant! You knew that I reap where I have not sown and gather where I scattered no seed? Then you ought to have invested my money with the bankers, and at my coming I should have received what was my own with interest. So take the talent from him and give it to him who has the ten talents. For to everyone who has will more be given, and he will have an abundance. But from the one who has not, even what he has will be taken away." (Source: Matthew 25:14-29, ESV).

How profound!

We are all born gifted people, and no one should deceive you that just because you are not an accomplished athlete then you cannot be a unique and accomplished engineer, architect, lawyer, accountant, speaker, writer, or whatever you desire to be. We all have hidden seeds of greatness, but it will take our own consented efforts to nurture the right kind of seeds which will manifest that inner greatness.

Most of us, our real talent may even not be in the profession we are pursuing today. Probably we are better actors than solicitors, or better still super writers than accountants. The process of discovering our inner talents is an ongoing one and we should not settle for less just because our academic papers presented a qualification seal on our foreheads. Honestly, the paper does not really define 'who we truly are', but rather presents a path of learning that we (or our parents) chose to pursue. Unfortunately, real education starts during or after we grab those papers.

Whilst doing my research for this book I stumbled upon an interesting story on *'themuse'*, an online destination for the next gen workforce to research companies and careers. The story relates to one Jeremy Schifeling who is the founder and Chief Nerd at Break into Tech, *a site for anyone who wants to land an awesome tech job, no matter their background.* Previously, Jeremy interned at Apple, hired at LinkedIn, and served as an executive at a VC-backed startup - all after starting his career as a kindergarten teacher!

According to his own write-up on *'themuse'*, Jeremy followed his first love when it was time to start his career. "Teaching kindergarten in Bedford–Stuyvesant, Brooklyn, felt like the perfect place to make a difference. But as with most things in life, a funny thing happened on the way to building my career: I found out that my passion and my expertise were not necessarily one in the same," he writes "I struggled to pull off the teaching thing, I found myself totally engrossed with all the techie aspects of my job: Building a classroom blog, teaching my students how to make videos, and even doing tech support on our ancient PCs. It was so clear that one of my co-workers finally pulled me aside and said: 'Jeremy, what the heck are you doing here? You should be in tech, man!'

"But as much as it hurt to realize that I wasn't cut out for (what I thought was) my dream job, I knew my colleague was right. And so, I set out to find my new dream job - one that combined both my

passions and my talents.

"Jeremy hence advises, when thinking about changing careers, it's tempting to focus on companies ("How cool would it be to work at Google?"). But please, resist that temptation and put yourself in the shoes of a recruiter, the gatekeeper who controls your occupational destiny. In my case, I knew I wasn't cut out to be a coder. But, given my passion for social justice and technology, I loved the idea of using tech to reach millions of people around the world. And so marketing was the perfect fit.

"And the best way to figure out what really matters is to look at the profiles of people who hold the job you want. If it turns out that every single career role model of yours has a certain degree or experience under her belt, chances are that's a good place for you to start".

He further writes, *"For me, that meant going back to grad school. Because even though I thought of an MBA as a degree for consultants and bankers, it turned out that pretty much all of the cool marketers I met at Apple, LinkedIn, and elsewhere had one. So, I went out and got an MBA too. (And for me, it was worth it.)"*

Get in the habit of intentionally creating time within your busy schedule to ponder on this reality of talents, whether there is something more to your life – and if at all there is something you would regret you haven't attempted to do in your lifetime. When the fear of financial struggle is passed (when you have made enough money) would you consider doing something greater, better, more challenging, more adventurous, beyond your job?

There is an adage that says "*the poor get poorer, and the rich get richer.*" I bet you've heard about it. But how true is this adage? I believe it is factual in every sense. And what's the principle behind it? It's the same one captured in the above parable of the talents.

People who are always cultivating their 'fields' and working out their gifts and talents will always have more. Same with those who continually understand that money creates more money. If all you know about money is spending and grabbing the next big thing, you will lose all you have and will probably become poor. Conversely, if you understand that money is nebulous and can work for you as much as you purpose, you will put it to work every time it hits your hand, and you stand a greater chance of becoming richer and financially prosperous.

Although, there is a reality that some people get rich using dubious means and they are brutal with the common citizens, it is also true that the world has a lot of better, candid, faithful, and trustworthy rich people. If all you do is castigate the rich because they appear to live larger than the average citizenry you will miss the bigger picture of wealth and prosperity. Instead of castigating the rich, a worthwhile use of your time would be to inquire and research how the rich got where they are, and somehow aspire to push through the boundaries of stagnation and reach out for your own greatness.

The only mistake we can make is staying idle and sleeping on the in-born greatness!

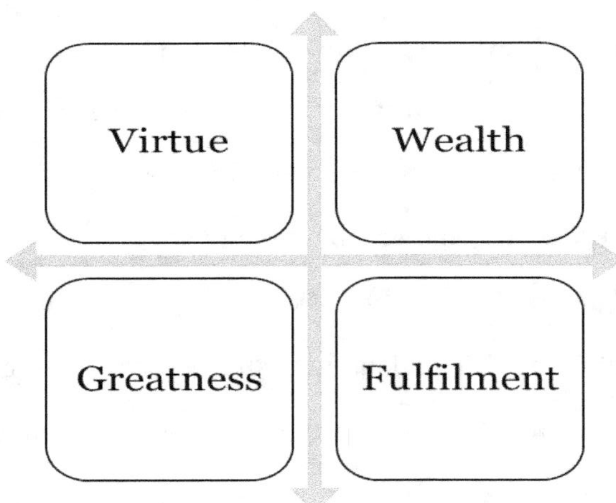

"Being intentional demands making a principled resolve that we will never accept mediocrity, complacency, and procrastination to inhabit our inner man. We will make deliberate choices to cultivate the seeds of greatness within us; and we will take care of our mental state, physical health, relationships, financial earnings, and generational mindset".

#don'tleaveyourmoneybehind

Focus

"Mastering your ability to stay on course"

3

Chapter 3: The Art of Focus

There are numerous things that can distract you from realizing your financial freedom. The usual pattern goes like this: the more money you get the more needs and responsibilities you have, not only in terms of what you truly need to spend on but also 'investment' opportunities that appear *too good to be true*. Unfortunately, most of such opportunities are mere infatuations driven by the media or a *'reliable report'* from a connection. With the knowledge and belief that your bank account is now liquid, you develop the tendency of having low risk evaluations, where you believe you can spend and lose without deep adverse impact and worry.

Nevertheless, if you soberly compound the losses, you will realize the molehill that develops from the numerous seemingly small losses. The random investments driven by fantasy and excitement will cost you a lot of your hard-earned money.

Since our core purpose is to ensure we earn enough, keep some, save more and invest – it is crucial to be aware of warped opportunities arising just to create unnecessary channels of spending. Although it's a neglected discipline, the art of focus is fundamental to the journey of preserving money in order to sustain our goals and help us leave the expat domain richer and wealthier.

How can we sustain focus with all this fever of consumerism?

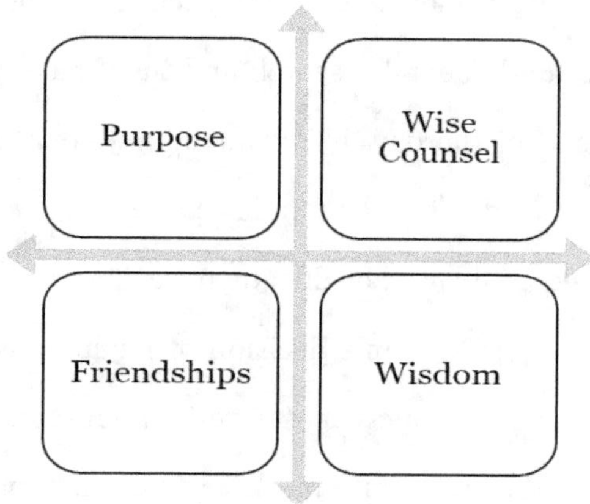

Purpose

Of course, we already discussed purpose, but we can't just let it go until it is hammered deep into the cranium. Purpose remains the biggest catalyst in the art of focus. It is the main compass that helps us identify any alien thoughts and opportunities that do not qualify within our 'long-haul agenda'. It is true and agreeable that some strange occurrences may still help propel us towards the main end; however, purpose also has a unique way of filtering such temporary considerations without hindering the main thing from being the main thing.

It is easy for us to identify those things that don't align with our principles, and we don't need to invest in those things, or to simply spend money on such stuff. For example, if you don't believe in an attractive and trendy investment opportunity such as cryptocurrencies, you simply need to do fundamental research and then make your personal decision. By the end of the day, it is your money. It is critical not to invest in something we don't understand because we may end up losing all our hard-earned cash merely due to pure ignorance. For some it could be property – just a simple decision of buying a condominium, villa, or mansion. Whatever one's chosen residential structure - without understanding how the real estate market works, they may still be hit badly and lose their money in the process. Bad deals are everywhere. You may even lose more cash through avoidable agency fees, insurance, taxes, city rates, and alien maintenance charges. Simply put, in the same market where others are minting cash, you may be melting yours.

Anything that does not fall within your life plan, your goals, your vision, shouldn't be on your list of investment ventures. Make sure you keep your money away from those things you less understand and are even less passionate about. I know that there is room for motivation plus expert advice – we will also address this one *over a cup of coffee*.

Sometimes it is not even about losing money on an investment. People lose money every day because of simple things such as food and clothes, as we will see in the chapter addressing *'shiny things'*. It is not abnormal to have an appetite for rare cuisines. Some of us may have a deep proclivity towards eating out and buying groceries from special shops. Sometimes we may even be coerced by friends to consistently go out. But if you have solid principles about these matters, you will quickly identify the adverse impact such decisions would have on your bank balance. You don't simply jump on every invitation. Excitement does not help us in the main agenda of 'keeping some, saving some, and investing some'.

A Solid Friendship Network

Finding yourself some good friends goes a long way in sustaining your accountability towards your set goals. Friends channel you towards that singular focal point of attaining financial freedom. Good friends don't celebrate or support your bad decisions or your losses. They are there to reprimand, encourage, and hold your hand when things get tough.

Although I didn't go through the painstaking process of defining 'friends', I presume we all understand what true friends are all about.

These should be people you are comfortable getting vulnerable to, and they sustain the privacy of deep matters discussed within the ancient pillars of friendship. This journey cannot be pursued together with naysayers and slanderers. You need to have some real brothers and sisters around you. Solid and deep people who are also pursuing their own worthwhile goals.

Friends should challenge you regarding your plans, investment goals, family values, spirituality, career, community, national agendas, among all the big-ticket items true friends discuss.

True friends equally open-up to you about their 'heart issues', and the accountability matrix becomes a double-pronged arsenal for continuous sharpening of our values. This is crucial because when you transgress from the committed life plan, you have someone who will give you the shots or prompts to get back on course. Personally, you also need to be vulnerable when you goof, and don't try to hide the transgressions from your accountability partner.

I understand that because of the confidentiality required for some personal plans we may opt to only confide in our spouses (especially for family matters); this is fine. At least as spouses you know that you have a singular agenda and you make sure to zoom-in on opportunities and goals without entertaining distractive thoughts and habits. This works for families that are truly moving together, in unison. This is how a family should be. Default settings.

However, there are other personal goals that may be classified as sharable with that one trusted friend. This is also commendable. Life should not be complex in such matters.

To achieve focus, say in investment plans, you may wish to bounce thoughts on your chosen accountability partner before you melt-in the cash. Be open about the opportunity – even if they shoot it down, their perspective will help you differentiate deep targets from fantasies. You may still choose to invest in that deal anyway but at least after looking at it from different angles. In the corporate domain this is called risk management. You get the opportunity of understanding most of the things that can hinder you from achieving your objectives, then you devise mitigation plans that will help you avoid or minimize the impact of an erroneous decision. You are good to go after this – whatever decision you make.

You may be the only person who understands what you need to do. You don't need to beat yourself. Whatever your friends advise, you are not bound to take their advice. Listening, however, is important.

Don't overstate your wisdom. Many people have gone through your path before and they are readily available to share notes on both pros and cons. Someone ever said, *"It is better to learn from counsel than experience."* You could save yourself from lots of headaches by choosing the former.

Seek the Advice of Experts

Once the money starts to grow, you may wish to seek the help of experts to advise on the ideal areas to invest or engage in. For example, if you want to buy property you need credible property experts or real estate agents who will direct you to the locations that will assure you of making a good profit on your investment, and people who will help you to grab affordable properties to ensure you don't dump all your nest in one risky venture. You don't just approach people who have never managed a property portfolio or even acquired their own real estate investment.

It is risky to leave your money in the hands of amateurs unless you are running an experiment. But I don't believe we have time to experiment with our hard-earned cash.

More so if you are planning to start stashing your cash away in your country of residence, or even another foreign location (which is not your home). You need to be guided by people who understand the terrain, or those who can differentiate the right from the left when it comes to striking deals on that soil.

Whether your business concept sounds as simple as trading household or clothing items, or as complex as selling automobiles or petroleum products, take some time to talk to people who have been in these trades for a while, attend business conferences, go to exhibitions, talk to as many people as possible. There is deeper wisdom in seeking counsel before you part ways with your money. Remember, we are talking about how *'not to leave your money behind,'* and one bad deal can trap you into leaving your money behind.

Even if you want to be an industry disruptor, it is easier to disrupt something that you know very well. The pioneers of the digital economy had to take time to study most of the stagnant manual processes of conducting traditional business before they could drop in 'some cool stuff' like social media platforms, data storage and sharing portals, software applications, e-commerce sites, and payment gateways. So, take time to understand what you want to disrupt, and see if your concept makes sense to you plus a few more credible and passionate people. Then you would be good to go. Even if you are working on a very unusual project which you believe no one should know about until you publish your stuff, you need to be prudent.

I know it takes a lot of humility to take advice. But taking advice may open you to many brilliant ideas or angles that you didn't even think about at the time of crafting your idea. If you talk to many business owners or entrepreneurs today, they will attest that their current businesses started off as something they thought 'that was it' until life happened. On the cards we have the likes of Facebook that started as a mere social site but has grown to become the world's largest advertising platform. I bet Mark and his friends didn't go out on the first day thinking *'we gonna make a killing with this campus social networking site'*.

In his world-class and generational masterpiece, *The Richest Man in Babylon*, George S. Clason lays out what he called the Five Laws of Gold. One of the Laws states, "Gold clingeth to the protection of the cautious owner who invests it under the advice of men wise in its handling".

In the book Clason also presents seven cures for a lean purse, one of which is *"Guard thy treasures from loss"*. He writes, *"Therefore, do I advise thee from the wisdom of my experiences: be not too confident of thine own wisdom in entrusting thy treasures to the possible pitfalls of investments. Better by far to consult the wisdom of those experienced in handling money for profit. Such advice is freely given for the asking and may readily possess a value equal in gold to the sum though considerest investing. In truth, such is the actual value if it save thee from loss".*

The above wisdom is also touted in this enduring statement that says, *"Where no counsel is, the people fall: but in the multitude of counselors there is safety"*. Proverbs 11:14 (KJV)

Close-out Unnecessary Noise – The Social Media Debacle

The world today is flooded with content, from social sites to a 'planetarium' of online news platforms, magazines, blogs, e-books, TV, Radio, podcasts, and massive streaming services. People keep on bombarding you with messages that don't even relate to you personally, or your environment, trade, career, or industry. But because you want to choose to be a consumer of information, everything will be dumped on you, especially if you are in the habit of subscribing to everything that pops up. This will make you become the easy target for all the media dumping, via emails and other online pages.

You can only focus on the core mission if you choose to close out all the nonsensical noise coming from the unwanted (or avoidable) sources. Quickly learn this art of maintaining focus by shutting down the media conduits and intentionally take some time out to detox your mind and create space for focused thinking. It only takes some stray words or messages to distract you from your goals. Some content is just toxic and depressing.

Unfortunately, when you are in the web of media, you may not even know how the content is influencing your thinking patterns. Marketing specialists understand that it is not necessarily the first food advert that will capture your sensory faculties to persuade you to buy a chicken burger. They know that it usually takes a few more billboards, YouTube videos, Facebook Ads, and then one more unsolicited email in your inbox. The next time you see the burger place your mind doesn't need any more introductions and convincing because subconsciously your mind was just waiting for this one opportunity to find the place, grab the burger, and devour it like a hungry lion.

This is the same way all other media bombardments work. They can suggest best ways to spend your money, where to go on holiday, what fitness program to get into, which schools to send your kids, which hotel to 'staycation' in, which car to replace your old 'moving item', which suits or dresses suit you best (what's in fashion today), and on and on the suggestions go.

Don't ever be deceived that social media, the marketing world, plus the electronic and print media houses are working for you. They are working on their own agendas, with you merely being one of the many millions, and indeed billions of pawns in their *game of thrones*.

Always be careful to choose your online teachers. Do not be a voluntary student to things that don't qualify within your biggest money saving, money keeping, and investing agenda. As much as this principle applies to the rest of our lives, it does massively impact our view on money and how to manage the same. Only allow information that solidifies your mission-oriented DNA.

I bet you have heard the social media ethos that says, "If you are not the customer then you are the product." This refers to the fact that if you are not paying for your social media subscriptions or indeed for any other online or software services. The service provider uses your free subscription to boost the numbers of the personal data held by their servers, and that data is their biggest asset and inventory. That's what makes them the millions, and your regular browsing is simply icing on the cake.

The equation gets complex if you have time to study and understand it. The data is their biggest asset because this is what they offer to their customers who care about any advertising numbers. Their social site and application data analytics are presented to their global customers to prove the available online market for their products and services. Once convinced, 'their customers' pay the companies to run adverts or market research on their sites. This is big money!

On the other hand, although you may be relishing your 'free subscription', the core customers start to bombard you with some tantalizing marketing bets, and most of you easily fall for these bets (although some of the marketed products and services may indeed be good for our existence); and ultimately you part away with some bucks. At this stage, you are no longer a free subscriber – you now become an indirect 'premium' subscriber. Essentially, it is easy for you to part ways with much larger sums of money, more than the ones you avoided paying for the subscription of the main social site.

Then there is another way you become a good pawn in the game of data and advertising; by virtue of being connected and obsessed with online scrolling, from looking at glittering photos of people you will never meet, to imbibing on gigabytes of random videos. Your consumption of heavy data firstly makes the primary data providers wealthy (like your mobile services provider), and subsequently what we call the 'content creators' (the people who produce and post the heavy videos you watch also end up getting a fair share of the spoils). Again, at this level of data consumption you are no longer a 'free subscriber' – you contribute to a massive global data market. I always say the wise ones are those who get busy producing content for 'online' consumers because they make money just by satisfying someone's eyes and ears.

If you reflect on your life, are you a content creator or a devoted data consumer?

Then there is another channel how you end up paying for these online subscriptions. Your Time. I believe this is the most expensive subscription cost component among all the other indirect costs mentioned above.

The time some of us spend on social sites and the many not-so-business-minded websites is baffling. Most mobile phones today have a function to show you the time spent on different activities. Try to check that out on your phone and see how many hours you spend on

Facebook, Instagram, Pinterest, TikTok, Twitter, Google+, WeChat, WhatsApp plus the numerous social sites developed by some smart kid across the sea. The time consumed in these stints is humongous for many people. The opportunity cost for the time being burnt are the many brilliant and generational ideas we could have been working on to develop our lives, our children, and our legacy for posterity.

Very few people use these sites for business connections, research, advertising, and learning. Very few smart ones spend less time on these sites, or no time at all.

Cal Newport, in his book, *'Deep Work: Rules For Focused Success In A Distracted World'*, discusses how professionals of today have started valuing quantity over quality; and how this has turned young professionals of today into puppets who try to indulge in extensive multitasking, dealing with multiple emails and projects. This prevents them from doing 'deep work'; which is focused work free from all other distractions. This also means that the professionals of today should sort out their priorities. This is adapted from Newport's own script about his publication.

Newport uses principles of psychology and neuroscience to enhance his points. He elaborates how to improve a person's cognitive abilities and how employers should encourage workers to not take shortcuts for completing projects. He claims that the best way to break away from the corporate race is to take a break from technology and social media and use some alone-time to rewind and introspect. Newport enforces the beliefs of a non-technophile to deliver work that is productive and efficiently delivered.

Beyond Newport's propositions, it is true that if you want to achieve audacious goals you cannot keep hanging on your social media pages and scrolling through unhelpful content for the whole day. Apart from wasting your precious time, the subtle most dangerous impact comes from the hidden intentions of the media posts - whether from your friends, random people, or professional marketers. A simple tweet on cars would see you running to your banker for a new automobile loan. A 'not-so-innocent' Facebook post from your friend showing their lounge in the background can see you quickly flipping through a home store magazine to see how you can also enhance your lounge (and probably to also start posting some nice Facebook posts). This is the world we are living in.

This mental pattern also relates to our earlier discussion on friendships. If your friendship profile is loaded with the excited buddies who keep on bombarding your social media home page with exotic trips, new cars, expensive homes and all the fun fare, you may one day find yourself owning a yacht (or at least a boat), mansion, and an A-List of trendy SUVs – all through painful bank loans!

Therefore, Newport's Deep Work does not only support the work and output notion, but also protects us from strange and harmful life's proclivities.

In a February 2020 Investopedia publication, "How *Facebook, Twitter, Social Media Make Money From You,"* Greg McFarlane writes:

An astounding number of people use social media each day, so it's a fair question to ask, "How do social media companies make money while offering so many free services?" As of December 2019, Facebook (FB) reports it has over 2.5 billion monthly active users, an increase of 8% year-over-year. Twitter (TWTR) reports it has 321 million monthly active users; while LinkedIn (MSFT) has about 260 million monthly active users. Such volume is the short answer to the question of how these companies are making money. But that doesn't tell the whole story. Here we explain exactly how the top powerhouse social media companies translate all that volume into cash.

The following are the key take-aways presented by the publication:

- *The primary way social media companies like Facebook and Twitter make money is through selling advertising.*

- *The concept of selling advertising while offering a free service is not new; television, newspapers, and media companies have been doing this long before social media companies existed.*

- *Facebook has over 2.5 billion monthly active users worldwide and estimates the average revenue per user (ARPU) in 2019 was $8.52.*

- *Facebook's ARPU comes primarily through profits earned from advertisers who use the platform to reach customers*

Note: *I opted to source information from Investopedia because they require writers to use primary sources to support their work. These include white papers, government data, original reporting, and interviews with industry experts. They also reference original research from other reputable publishers where appropriate. The quoted data is mainly derived from the listed companies' fiscal results and published market results.*

Seeking the Truth and Finding Wisdom

There are too many things happening around the world. As long as you understand who you are, as a human being; how you came to earth (others prefer to call it the green dot), and why you are here –

it becomes apparent that God made everything and we exist to fulfil a greater purpose far above what our eyes can see. This realization keeps us humble and sane throughout this sojourn on earth.

In our quest for focus and significance, we don't want to be erroneously engulfed in earthly matters that are not beneficial to our mission; we want to exert our influence and to deploy our time and resources on things that will have the highest impact and give us the greatest Return on Investment (ROI). Fortunately, those things are pretty much already prescribed for us by the Creator. We don't need to go running around trying to define God's purpose for our lives. If you believe in the existence of God like I do, then you should be having a reference point from which you get your source of inspiration.

My own source of inspiration is the written word from the Bible and the confidence that I can directly pray to God (or petition) regarding life's challenges and opportunities. When I find myself losing focus, I just quickly turn to God for guidance, revelation, and clarity on both short-term and long-term goals. And the good news is that I have never been disappointed after surrendering my pursuits and 'what we call hustle' to God.

You know, all things may be permissible, but not all things are beneficial. We need to know how to navigate the options of life and be able to follow a strict or predefined pattern. We should seek enduring goals that if we attain, we are going to achieve more value – beyond the earthly treasures; there should be a wider impact on other people's lives, our nation, and our posterity. There should also be a tangent to the eternal reality of life after our sojourn on earth. The art of focus is not complete until we are able to yield exponential returns, now, and throughout eternity.

People who are driven by something higher and greater than themselves are bound to impact the world in massive proportions, and to live a mark that will outlive them on the earth. We can attest of the people we have known in our generation and those who lived large in generations past. To mind comes names like Nelson Mandela, Martin Luther King Jr., Mahatma Gandhi, Desmond Tutu, Mother Theresa, Leonardo Da Vinci, Muhammad Ali, Kwame Nkrumah, Henry Ford, Albert Einstein, Nikola Tesla, Sandford Fleming, Alexander Graham Bell, Walt Disney, Orville & Wilbur Wright, and many others.

Today we can talk of the many innovators, creators, entrepreneurs, and talented souls who have shaped our world and the way we navigate daily activities, from Elon Musk, Steve Jobs, Jeff Bezos, Larry Page, Bill Gates, Mark Zuckerberg, Pele (Edson Arantes do Nascimento),

Lionel Messi, Cristiano Ronaldo, Maya Angelou, Aliko Dangote, Chimamanda Ngozi Adichie, Jack Andraka, and many others.

I know I have been selective in presenting the above names, but my main objective is bringing to memory what these great men and women have done for the world. Through God's provision and wisdom mere men and women can devise quantum solutions to the globe's endless problems. Hence in our quest for meaning and abundance, we must always remember that there is work to be done beyond the money. We may be hiding the next big inventors of our time, either within ourselves or at least within our homes and communities. Beyond invention, our earnings can go a long way in alleviating poverty and suffering around the world, or at least to sponsor and finance worthwhile causes for the betterment of humanity and our posterity.

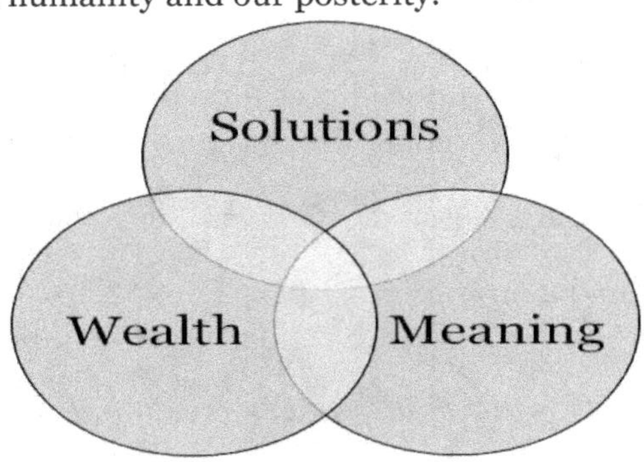

Focus may be one of the most ignored ingredients of success, but its absence always leads to chaos and human failure.

#don'tleaveyourmoneybehind

The Shiny Things

"Not all that glitters is meaningful"

4

Chapter 4: Don't Chase Every Shiny Thing

When you come to a new country, there are usually lots of shiny things; lots of offers and a beckoning lifestyle of grandeur. And it is not uncommon for expats to get exorcised with a deceitful feeling of success even before the bucks start trickling in. I understand there are seasoned expats who come into new places after having worked in multiple countries and are gurus in navigating the basic fantasies of this life. They understand how to settle quickly and focus on the big-ticket items, including local wealth transfer. I have worked with so many senior consultants who were probably getting into this space for their third or fourth international stints, and most of them came with loads of life savings and investments.

At the time we were grappling with bank loans to get our cars, these consultants easily walked into car showrooms to pull out the kind of cars they 'love' to drive; not 'what they could afford to drive'. It is a different consumer perspective when you have a dense bank account.

But I am talking about the newbies – the ones on the starting line of the expat sojourn. When you are new there is a sense of freedom that comes with getting an overseas opportunity and you are excited at the prospect of making *'abnormal'* amounts of money.

Unfortunately, if you missed-out on the first part of finding your purpose and setting a personal vision, you get trapped in a bunch of voices that give you narratives about how and what you need to do, how to lead your life, plus all the good loans you can get, and even what you need to spend on. The type of life included. You even get offers based on where you live or the outlook of your account. Remember the bank people can see how much is being *melted* into your bank account monthly. Hence some people easily commit to the housing solutions that come with pomp like a villa (or some sizeable mansion) that would define their lifestyle and social position in the expat community. If your company gives you that cozy villa, rejoice and praise your way to the bank. Live your days in gladness; absolutely!

For liquid economies, the banks are more than ready to finance your V8 SUV merely on the basis of your first salary. It is incredible! This is the car you've been dreaming about for the past 10 years and the bank just hands over the required budget without blinking.

This is something I observed in the Arabian Gulf States – the GCC. With my given monthly package, I could easily walk into a bank and ask them to finance my hunger for a new Range Rover! This is something that would never happen back home in Malawi. The bank would have first asked me about my salary, then some tangible collateral (like real estate) and some guarantee from my employer. And, of course, the qualifying loan would not be sufficient to coerce the Range Rover from its ambient showroom. No. I would probably be given something that could afford me a KIA Rio or equivalent – otherwise a reconditioned Mercedes Benz Kompressor or second hand BWM 5-Series.

The financing opportunity is what causes excitement and a rare quest to just prove that you can finally pull that machine across the roads of the East. Amazing feeling.

One reality though, once the machine hits the road, the bank loan also hits your liability statement, and in a twinkle of an eye you are now a debtor listed in the books of the bank with a good credit ranging between US$101,000 to US$211,000 - being the price range of the 2023 Range Rover according to the Automobile Website, Edmunds.

Sometimes you easily justify that the bank loan is obtained at a very low interest rate compared to back home, and the fuel cost would not break the bank account, right? So, you just go on and get the loan and walk into a showroom with pomp, like a king. Then the next step comes through, the friends that start pulling themselves around you become the big guns – loaded men and women. As the adage goes, *like attracts like*. Hence everyone with 'big everything' gets attracted to you. The next thing is that you start learning all the ways to live large - the nice restaurants around town, the best jewelry and fashion stores, the kind of supermarkets 'they' go to, and how they spend their weekend. Doesn't sound so bad, does it?

If all these symbiotic attractions happen too quickly, for many new expats, the realization that your salary has not been supporting the newly-adopted lifestyle comes late and your eyes open to the reality that it's been the bankers behind all the funding requirements, from the shiny cool car, the villa, the suits, the perfumes, the jewelry, the food, the trips, the latte, and all the simple things of life. Credit cards can do all this plus some overdrafts, coupled with personal loans that hit your bank account without even knowing why they are there. Life has amazing ways! Did you really have a plan on how you want to use your money? Or is the use of numerous shiny things meeting your life goals?

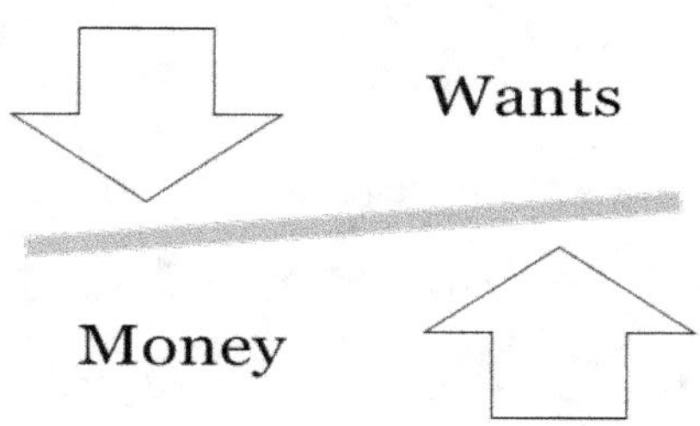

Be Wary of Consumerism

Consumerism is the idea that increasing the consumption of goods and services purchased in the market is always a desirable goal and that a person's wellbeing and happiness depend fundamentally on obtaining consumer goods and material possessions. In an economic sense, it is related to the Keynesian idea that consumer spending is the key driver of the economy and that encouraging consumers to spend is a major policy goal. From this point of view, consumerism is a positive phenomenon that fuels economic growth. *(Adam Hayes – Consumerism: Investopedia, Mar 18,2021).*

Kerryn Higgs, an Australian writer, historian and the author of *"Collision Course: Endless Growth on a Finite Planet,"* published on BBC Future an adapted article titled *"How the world embraced consumerism"*. She wrote, "The notion of human beings as consumers first took shape before World War One but became commonplace in America in the 1920s. Consumption is now frequently seen as our principal role in the world.

People, of course, have always "consumed" the necessities of life – food, shelter, clothing – and have always had to work to get them or have others work for them, but there was little economic motive for increased consumption among the mass of people before the 20th

Century.

Quite the reverse: frugality and thrift were more appropriate to situations where survival rations were not guaranteed. Attempts to promote new fashions, harness the "propulsive power of envy," and boost sales multiplied in Britain in the late 18th Century. Here began the "slow unleashing of the acquisitive instincts," write historians Neil McKendrick, John Brewer, and J H Plumb in their influential book on the *commercialization of 18th-Century England*, when the pursuit of opulence and display first extended beyond the very rich.

"But, while poorer people might have acquired a very few useful household items – a skillet, perhaps, or an iron pot – the sumptuous clothing, furniture, and pottery of the era were still confined to a very small population."

Nevertheless, Consumerism increases debt levels which in turn results in mental health problems like stress and depression. Trying to follow the latest trends when you have limited resources can be very exhausting to the mind and body. Consumerism forces people to work harder, borrow more and spend less time with loved ones. Consumerism gets in the way of fruitful relationships. It affects the overall well-being of people negatively in the long run since research has proven that people don't get valuable and long-lasting fulfilment from materialism – *(Mark Scott: What You Need to Know About Consumerism, Swift Money – 24 Apr,2017).*

Remember, when you were coming overseas, your plan was to make some money for those deep life goals, unless this wasn't thought through from the start. However, if you are not careful and you just jump on the fast train, all your money ends up being hooked up by the baits – the cars, the houses, the trips, the entertainment, the unknown escapades, et al. and some baits may be justifiable. For example, a good expensive school. Kids deserve some good world-class education. Nevertheless, schooling options should also go through a proper screening process to avoid falling for a brand.

There are lots of lessons in numerous books on how to define beneficial and non-beneficial expenditures or purchases; also known as differentiating assets from liabilities. Robert Kiyosaki is one of the famous proponents of this teaching which he originally published in his book *'Rich Dad Poor Dad'.* The five big ideas from Kiyosaki's book are presented below:

- *The poor and the middle-class work for money. The rich have money work for them.*

- *It's not how much money you make that matters. It's how much money you keep.*
- *Rich people acquire assets. The poor and middle class acquire liabilities that they think are assets.*
- *Financial aptitude is what you do with money once you make it, how you keep people from taking it from you, how to keep it longer, and how you make money work hard for you.*
- *The single most powerful asset we all have is our mind.*

For this book, and in my own words, **an asset is an investment, purchase, or acquisition that brings more value either through use or earning you more money.** A liability is also an acquisition or expenditure that feeds on what you have. It depletes and devours your money. So, a nice car can be a liability if it keeps on guzzling more money from you through maintenance and enhancements. And similarly, a nice villa, although having a fixed monthly rental amount may be a liability because of the heavy requirement for you to sustain the landscape, the swimming pool, city rates, the maintenance of more rooms and the labor fees to sustain all the underlying jobs, including cleaning. When you are getting the mammoth place, you need to understand the technicalities of maintaining that place.

Please hear me right. I am not against people's progress and the idea of living large. If my bank account is dripping cash, I would be the first one to jump into the most awesome place on earth. In this book we are talking about life's principles that will secure your future by securing your money first. It is important to understand that the core issue here is timing. We need to appreciate seasons of our lives and growth – there is a time to stay put, learn, save, grow and then you can live as large as you want. Wisdom demands the fact that we learn to wait for the perfect time to expand our territories of both influence and affluence. Hence, if you are already at the required stage of affluence, live large with no apology- you deserve it.

The Book of Ecclesiastes *(NIV)* presents times and seasons as follows:

"There is a time for everything, and a season for every activity under heaven:

a time to be born and a time to die, a

time to plant and a time to uproot, a

time to kill and a time to heal,

a time to tear down and a time to build, a

time to weep and a time to laugh,

a time to mourn and a time to dance,

a time to scatter stones and a time to gather them, a

time to embrace and a time to refrain,

a time to search and a time to give up,

a time to keep and a time to throw away, a

time to tear and a time to mend,

a time to be silent and a time to speak, a

time to love and a time to hate,

a time for war and a time for peace."

It is fundamental for us to deeply understand the season we are going through in order to silence the demands of life which are meant to be attained in a different season of our life. It is beneficial to indeed take one day at a time when it comes to matters of getting, keeping, and investing money. Everyone has their own journey and there is no need to be heavily persuaded by those who may appear to have attained great wealth ahead of others. It is their season, and ours will come too. Don't stress.

A Snippet on Pets

Another crucial but discretionary expense is pet maintenance. If you are a big pet lover but know that pet food may not be as cheap as bread and chicken, it's better to delay welcoming one into your home until you are ready to lovingly own and take care of the pet, properly. In my expat years I have seen numerous pet lovers who ended up abandoning their adorable pets in the city streets when they had to go home unexpectedly due to some emergency, for example after an abrupt lay-off.

Pets also attract significant costs during travel, be it on vacation or business trips, especially for single expats or those working on non-family roles as they either have to travel with the pet or hire special services in case they don't have family or friends to take care of the pet. Depending on the weight of your pet, uniqueness, the destination, the flight carrier, or indeed whether you are travelling with a 'service' or standard pet, the usual 'baggage' rates would range between US$100 and US$450 as evidenced in 2021 from airline sites across Qatar

Airways, Fly Emirates, British Airways, American Airlines, among others. Service pets may be allowed into the cabin for free, again depending on the airline you are using.

However, according to *Travel+Leisure* Online, the fees for traveling with a pet can quickly add up, even before you leave home. The preparation for traveling with your best furry friend should include heading to the vet for a checkup, especially since airlines can require an up-to-date health certificate signed by a veterinarian Additionally, Consumer Reports recommend looking into a microchip for your pooch just in case he or she gets loose in a new area. The cost of inserting a microchip would typically cost about $45, according to Petfinder.

Once all the background care is complete, it's time to think about how you'll get from point A to point B. *Travel+Leisure* further advises that Airlines typically charge a $100 to $125 one-way fee to bring your dog in the cabin. And, if you want your pet to fly in the cabin, you'll need to purchase an airline-compliant pet carrier, which can cost from $30 up to $250, according to Consumer Reports.

Just for the record, due to the complexities and consideration of pet size, destination, and all the factors mentioned above, for your pet to fly in the cargo hold sometimes the cost may get well over US$1,000, hence crucial to conduct sufficient research before bringing your pets along to an expat location, or indeed before acquiring one in your current location.

The other major pet maintenance cost comes from veterinary services. Definitely, if you desire to own a pet it is important to ensure you also understand the cost of sustaining the pet's well-being. There are numerous online sources and books on the subject, and it would do you (and the targeted pets) great justice to scour the internet for periodic budgetary planning.

According to *DocShop*, a US-based online portal that connects people with experienced healthcare professionals, each animal has distinctive veterinary needs based on its species, breed, pre-existing conditions, personality, age, and medical history. In general, the AVMA (American Veterinary Medical Association) estimates that animal caretakers typically spend the following on medical treatments and services for their pets (per year) as of 2021:

- **Dogs:** $227 per animal and $378 per household (since many owners have more than one pet)
- **Cats:** $90 per animal and $191 per household

- **Birds:** $14 per animal and $33 per household

Smaller pets like hamsters and rabbits may cost between $30 and $90 per animal each year, while fish, frogs, and reptiles typically require between $20 and $80 per year in veterinary assistance, although some may need none. Your vet costs will typically increase as your pet ages, especially if your animal is prone to congenital conditions (for example, some types of purebred dogs tend to develop certain orthopedic issues as they get older).

According to DocShop, the above average costs need to be considered considering the other common pet-upkeep costs as veterinary costs are not the only expenses associated with animal ownership and caretaking. You will also need to budget for your animal's food, water, bedding, toys, leash, litter box, and any other items. While not technically medical costs, many of these products help ensure the pet's wellbeing and comfort.

Talking about pet food, Jenna Stregowski, writing for Spruce Pets Online provides some key information, stating for example, that feeding your dog a high-quality dog food typically costs somewhere from $20 to $60 per month ($250 to $700 per year). Food expenses vary based on the size and energy level of your dog as well as the quality of the food. Furthermore, special foods, like veterinary therapeutic diets or freshly-made special-order food, may cost $100 or more a month.

Overall, monthly costs for taking care of your pet dog may range well between US$125 and US$824, while the annual costs between US$1,500 and US$9,900 - covering food and treats, toys, beds, lashes & collars, grooming, routine veterinary care, preventive medication & supplements, training classes & resources, dog walking, and pet sitters or boarding.

In summary, you simply need to be prepared for a high life. As much as you would be an avid pet lover like I was some years back (*and still one at heart*), you need to take tactical steps before flying your pets to an overseas expat location. Take calculated decisions to ensure unforeseen pet maintenance costs don't drain your bank account dry.

A Snippet on Cars

There will always be expats earning much higher than you, just like you will always have some earning far much lower than you. It is not a race. Our proclivities and spending appetites will always vary depending on the season of our life or our financial ability to sustain the unique spending habits.

Hence, when it comes to the choice of car we want to drive, this book is not about encouraging everyone to drive modestly or to abandon the wonderful luxurious experience. No matter the noise (or sincere concerns) from frugality campaigners, rich and wealthy people don't really qualify for some of the mundane savings advice that we try to blow over the roof-tops. That's why this book is written for a specific audience – those who left home to pursue a worthwhile financial freedom goal. Those who have not yet made it in the books of the wealthy, or at least still trailblazing a path towards that direction, on the quest to change their family narrative. It is more than about saving money. It is a higher calling.

Coming back to the snippet, when buying a car, it is worthwhile to consider the baseline functionalities of a motor vehicle, including transportation (to move from Point A to Point B), safety, security, comfort, entertainment & leisure, etc. depending on why you need a car. Once you are clear on these fundamentals, the next step becomes much easier.

Secondly, you need to consider personal preferences in terms of car type, model, and brand. For example, if you have a big family, you may need an SUV instead of a Sedan. If you are a 'territorial master' you may need to get a 4x4 with a proven track record of surviving the jungles, deserts, and every rough terrain, such as the Toyota Land Cruiser. I am not marketing the brand, just being frank.

If you are single or a small family with no passion for the outskirts of the city, you may survive with a nice Sedan with due consideration to the safety and performance features.

Thirdly, you need to consider the cost of 'your preferences', and whether you need to buy a brand-new or second-hand (used) car.

According to my personal experience and numerous consumer reports, every new car loses massive showroom value soon after hitting the tarmac. Based on a *carsdirect.com* publication, a new car depreciates or loses value almost immediately after you drive it off a dealer's lot. As a quick rule of thumb, a car will lose between 15% and 20% of its value each year according to *Bankrate.com.* A car in its second year will be worth 80% to 85% of its first-year value and a car in its third year will be worth 80% to 85% of its second-year value.

The publication continues to highlight that the amount or level at which the vehicle depreciates varies depending on the make, model, year, type, and other factors associated with the car.

A simple thing like the color of your car may have significant influence of the resale value; for example, neutral colors such as black, white and grey retain higher values than customized colors such as 'wine pink' or 'primrose'. Choose strange colors only when you know that, truly, this experience is for you, and you alone. You don't really care whether someone will help you offload this moving baggage somewhere down the line.

On whether you need to get a new or used car, this depends on multiple personal factors. Based on my experience, the following factors should be considered before jumping into any commitment:

- **The purchase cost** – does it look reasonable based on your annual earning capacity? For example, for someone with gross earnings of US$7,500 per month, it wouldn't lock wise (on face value) to commit to a US$75,000 4 years bank loan.

- **Financing costs** (if you are getting a loan). If we use the above example: Getting a US$75,000 automotive loan at 7% annual bank interest with a payment period of 4 years, means the monthly repayment would be around US$1,800 with a total targeted interest of US$11,200 within the committed 4 years, resulting in a total payment of around US$ 97,600. If this is the targeted motor vehicle financing cost, the concern should be whether you will also manage to have equivalent or more savings and investment sums during the same 4-year period, or whether your sole life mission will be the debt repayment.

Although the car will have a residual or resale value (say 30% of the original cost), there are other maintenance, registration, and insurance costs that will have an adverse effect on such residual value. So if you think the car will have a resale value of around US$22,500 after the 4 years, if you do simple arithmetic to deduct the annual maintenance, registration and insurance charges, you may realize that the real net benefit upon selling the car would be below US$15,000, including the opportunity cost for not investing those additional costs in something worthwhile.

- **Your expected job tenure** and the assessed risks, especially job and economic stability. For example, if you only have a two-year contract, it would be unwise to get into a 4-year financing arrangement. Also, you would be too optimistic to buy a US$75,000 brand new car (on a loan) during a crisis for example. It does not mean that every economic indicator spells doom on your life; however, calculated risks should be expected to cover such environmental considerations.

- **Maintenance costs** comparison between a new car and its second-hand equivalent. Beyond the reality of a new or used car, maintenance costs are usually driven by the car type and model. For example, most European brands are known to attract higher maintenance costs compared to their Asian competition. This is not even a matter of dwindling or spiking sales for one over the other brands. It is a reality of life between those who have already made it in life versus those who are still pushing across the 'poverty' lines.

It is important to inquire from existing car owners of similar brands and models on how much they spend on maintaining their Range Rover, BMW, Mercedes Benz, KIA, Toyota, Honda, Tesla, Daihatsu, Mazda, or Nissan, among the wide motor vehicle spectrum.

If you need my advice, I recommend you first look at your bank account, and remember the financial targets we discussed in the earlier pages, and then see whether the expected annual maintenance costs for a used BMW X5 will help you attain that specific financial goal.

If you are getting a new car, of course, you will get some service warranty and free services in the initial year and hence looks very manageable; nevertheless, you need to be prepared for any ancillary costs that can be understood through simple online research or inquiry from other car owners, especially within the same brand and model lines.

- **Whether you are more concerned about the resale value** or if you have any plans to take the car back to your home country. If you are buying an expensive car, you would automatically get concerned about the resale value as you would not want to lose the residual car value after only using it for a few years, as indicated above.

  Depending on your location, some car brands retain higher values than others. For example, in the Middle Eastern Gulf Countries (or the GCC) where I have lived for the longest time, Toyotas and Nissans are known to retain higher values than European Brands, hence it is common to see a 5 years' Mercedes Benz going at a much lower price than its equivalent Toyota or Nissan model. Hence if the exit plan is a resale, you know exactly what brand preserves your money. Otherwise, if the plan is to drive well and 'enjoy the fruits of your labor', resale value is never your major concern.

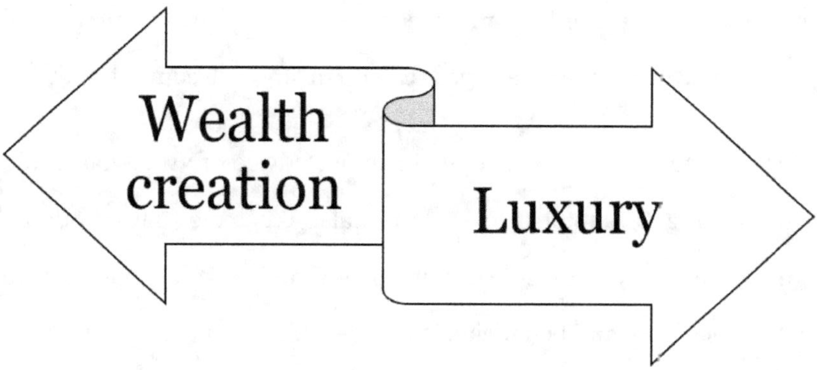

A Snippet on Housing

For most expats, housing is the major cost element on the monthly budget, usually the first or only second to educational fees. The general rule is to ensure your monthly rentals are maintained at or below 25-30% of your gross salary. From my experience, I would say, if it is practical to your circumstances, even target the rentals to be within the 15-20% bracket of your gross pay. This approach cushions your net savings from the effects of tax and other monthly fixed costs such as utilities, home support, and some unavoidable subscriptions. You know the type that clings to you (*literally*).

This means if your monthly gross pay (pre-tax) is US$10,000, US$2,000 (20%) will be the maximum you can pay to a landlord. Period. This will mean that for an annual gross pay of US$120,000, US$24,000 will be the maximum commitment towards your annual rentals. Now you can see what a year can do to any cost-commitment.

If you were stuck with the general consumer advice of 30%, you would end up locking US$36,000 towards rentals! Trust me, the additional US$12,000 is a lot of money especially if you can invest it somewhere in something scalable and beneficial. Whatever this means to you.

I love *talking in numbers*. If you use percentages or emotions in deciding your financial future, it does not feel the same way when you look at the *numerical impact*.

When it comes to choosing a home, beyond the price tag, it is important to look at functionality rather than only looking at location, ambience, quality, status, among the many other factors. By functionality I mean what rooms-fittings-spaces-lightings-things you need to have in your home. For example, if you love gardening you may say you will get a villa with a backyard, or an apartment with a balcony because you can't just live without growing your own plants. Or if you have a pet (or pets) you may need wider spaces to allow for a fair human and animal interaction around the home.

If you have kids, your decisions will usually be driven by whether you have a community around you that can sustain happy and playful moments for the kids. You basically need to be around other families with kids who can reduce the stress of driving around town searching for friends – or literally bothering the only (unyielding and tired) friend to release their kids to play with yours. I have been there seen that!

Once you have honestly looked at your personal needs, you may now need to look at whether your preferred home can be found in the most convenient location of town. Talking to several expats, I have come to realize that most people choose their homes based on a few key factors – including distance to work, schools, markets, or places of worship.

After taking the simple preference analysis, you can now bounce back to the question of cost. Consider the following questions:

- Can you find your preferred home within the 20% bracket of your gross pay?

- Will your basic preferences be met at the specific location or with the type of 'affordable' existing homes?

- How will your housing preferences affect your savings or investment agenda?

- Can you make reasonable compromises on the savings or investments target for the sake of your mental and physical health (or comfort)?

- Do you need to buy your own furniture or are you okay with used furniture?

- Are your housing and location choices having any positive or negative effects on the present and future lives of your children? This question is critical in view of mental health issues that are also having a heavy effect on many expat children due to loneliness, limited friendships, identity crisis (lack of clear belonging), language barriers, inadequate kids play, among other key factors.

After sober reflections and sincere advice from friends or real estate agents, you would be in a better position to make personal choices that suit your circumstances. When all is said and done, only you can make a decision that is fully based on 'loving yourself'.

Such a decision may lead you to increase your gross pay percentage bracket for rental costs with a reasonable rationale to safeguard the safety of your kids for example.

As well-said by *Expat.com*, keep in mind that rent prices do not necessarily reflect the quality of housing. In city centers, for example, you are more likely to find modern and luxury flats that are incredibly pricey. As you move further from the city centre, but not necessarily in the outskirts, you might find some beautiful, detached houses with a garden – which are better for families with young children.

The *Expats.com* advice is true and does resonate with many experienced expats. Unfortunately, the realization that you have been paying for excessive avoidable costs usually comes after you've already spent 2 to 3 years in some old and dusty apartment within the city centre. A simple stroll within a 10 to 20 kilometers radius can manifest more beautiful and competitive living environments.

When it comes to choosing furnished or unfurnished accommodation, I always advise newcomers to first explore the city from an affordable furnished apartment before investing too much in their own furniture, unless your company arrangements include corporate housing and furnishings. Even in cases where the company provides some form of on-boarding allowance, it is wiser to wait (*and understand the new terrain*) before wallowing in any form of home shopping. A couple of months' delay may reveal a lot of stuff about the new place which can result in massive cost savings plus allowing you to choose a better home.

For expats with short term contracts, it is commendable to adopt the first approach of staying in furnished accommodations to avoid heavy investments in unnecessary furnishings. Experience has shown that furniture has a similar value retaining period like motor vehicles. For example, a nice IKEA chest of drawers worth US$300 would easily go at US$100 after a mere 6 months! That's the reality of expat life.

Unless you are someone seeking permanent residence, it is also prudent to consistently have an inner counselor who reminds you that this place is not home. It is possible to reconcile the reality that your best days are being spent now with the fact that you are not a citizen of this land.

Live well, live large – but don't burn all you get for the sake of temporary comfort. I guess that's my central message in these pages.

A contrary message would read – *"it is better to buy your own furniture to avoid paying excessive rental costs due to the furniture provision".* This point has some elements of truth, but not the whole truth; hence it should be viewed and followed based on your unique circumstances as indicated above. Buying your own furniture means spending money, and you need to soberly consider the effect of that type of expenditure, and whether the depreciation effect (or loss in value of your furniture) is still better than getting a furnished accommodation. The critical actions should be deep-thinking and seeking advice from people who understand this stuff. These simple actions will save you money and avoidable mistakes.

Many times, through focused and intentional search for competitive prices, I have lived in newly furnished accommodations which had much lower rentals than old, unfurnished, and unattractive accommodations. However, I have also learnt that owning your furniture and getting a cheaper but cleaner unfurnished apartment or villa is usually the best choice for long-haul expats. Whatever final decision you make, always focus on controlling the costs from the source, for example by:

- Adopting a hybrid furnishing approach of getting new items on selected stuff and searching secondhand sites for the rest. In my own experience I've known expats who would always buy new beds and sofas but don't mind getting used dining sets, kitchen equipment, electronics, and random cabinets. Somehow the bed is always better when new; *I can't expound beyond this point.*

- Get a furnished apartment or house if the envisaged baseline cost plus furniture premium is still below your chosen gross pay percentage, and if this option frees you from the chaos of choice and avoidable expenditure.

A Snippet on Schools

I can talk about schools forever!

Firstly, almost all expats with kids would wish they made the international move on a compensation package that included school fees for their kids. But it never works this way all the time. Or I should say it is not always the case because:

- People join companies at different grades or levels, e.g., not everyone would join a company at a director or vice president level. Some professionals have to join at an entry level position – and the reality is that very few companies cover school fees for lower levels. It's just how life is patterned.

- People join different employers. Regardless of the industry, some companies just don't pay school fees. That's it. No discussions. No additional rationale. You get what you signed up for.

Depending on your prospective employer, whether in your first stint or when changing jobs abroad, it is important to always assess the industry equivalents of your pay grade and ensure your experience and qualifications are also reasonably paired with your targeted role.

I appreciate there could be employers with obvious biases on your education (especially your university degree – or which university you went to), or where you come from – however, these biases should not preclude you from presenting your true worth and demanding what you believe you deserve for that position.

If the company has a policy to sponsor school fees, it's a massive and rare blessing which should be embraced with zest and gratitude. Dipping school costs from your own bank account is literally a showstopper for many expats. Again, I have been there, seen that.

Talking to my expats network, most people confessed that school fees has had the effect of broadening their bank loans and credit cards just to keep their families afloat. It is a common story for most expat families living without educational support. This is why this discussion is crucial when you are getting into a senior international role.

For junior roles, the absence of educational support should not entail a default rejection of the job offer, unless survival is assessed at an impossible level depending on the applicable cost of living in the country. If you have young kids (below kindergarten age), you can survive until they get to school age. Who knows life will happen between now and then? It could be that your company may start supporting the fees component (if policy allows), or you may have gained sufficient international experience to command better-paying opportunities.

Most well-paid expats started from the bottom-up. Matters of compensation should be viewed through the lens of experience and time. It is unfair to oneself when you stress over salary comparisons against people who have spent tens of years in the profession and industry. My modest professional experience has shown that time clarifies a lot of questions. Take time to learn, rest, work hard, push the qualification boundaries, and deserve the progressive benefits. When you keep on becoming a better version of yourself, even if your present employer fails to acknowledge your value, one of these days another employer or business partner will do, and that will be your turning point.

As long as you are working on yourself, something has to give!

Regarding the choice of schools, high level screening usually broadens the question of the curriculum, nationalities, location, management, teachers, facilities, and costs. For example, on curriculum, if your preference is the British or American curriculum, or IGCSE versus IB Schools, this clarification alone sieves through a bunch of schools falling outside your target. In addition, parents go through the pain of selecting schools with a known history of churning future graduates from Oxford, Harvard, Cambridge, Stanford, MIT, Yale and other Ivy League Universities.

Since school fees take up a bigger component of your gross pay (just like accommodation, and mostly more), schools should also be chosen based on your "deep why". It is important to be clear what 'quality education' means to you, and why you are pushed towards specific schools. Also be aware of unnecessary peer pressure. It is not good enough to send your kids to an expensive school just because most of your friends or workmates send their kids there. You may also get alternative online schooling until you are able to transition your kids into a physical school. Several expat families have successfully raised their kids through the online schooling system. It just depends on personal preferences, research, knowledge, and timing.

My 12 years expat experience, as of the time of authoring this book, has taught me that focusing on the school's principles, ethics, environment, and teachers' commitment yields a higher reward than fame and costs. The most expensive school does not necessarily mean they will produce princes and princesses. You will be surprised to know that some expensive schools are usual culprits in producing rascals due to failed ethical and disciplinary standards. These are the type of schools that only provide a platform for kids from rich families to showcase their wealth (instead of enduring personal worth).

So, before you get on the bandwagon of chasing the most expensive school (which is not a problem in itself), it is always better to assess the behavioral attributes of the school system. Spend time getting feedback from current parents and those of some alumni if you can. Otherwise, online sources can also be the best repository of parents and expert reviews. Google reviews can be trusted if you have a finer eye on discretion.

For comical purposes, some of us were groomed by public, community, and mission schools that, till date, have not appeared on any radar of the global economy. We didn't have the privilege of being dropped at school in a Maserati or using touch screens to make Grade 2 presentations. Somehow, we still came out fine by the grace of God. The same papers gained on the foundation of these schools have allowed us to get international opportunities and to spearhead commendable innovations in our industries. All this within a budget that barely covers the learning cost of a second-year grader!

I do not talk about my simplistic history with neglect to the tremendous educational advancement made in the modern world, including the progress in blockchain technology, artificial intelligence, and machine learning, but rather to show us that a successful life is still possible through simple academic routes. Our kids can always find a conduit towards a higher level of academic excellence at graduate or post-graduate level.

This is also not in any way meant to demean the massive impact that an Ivy League degree would have on our children's resume; however, there is also a reality that not all life's achievements were attained by students who spent US$15,000 a year in intermediate schools, nor US$80,000 per year in an Ivy League University. Chance and unique opportunities happen to them all.

There is also a life reality that beyond sponsoring your children's school fees, you need to ensure your own savings and investments are looking good enough to sustain your life after retirement. A healthy expenditure balance will ensure parents don't place the burden on their kids to do the heavy educational work with the expectation of financially supporting their parents for the rest of their lives. *This is not commendable.*

Why Think About These Matters?

If you don't develop a feasible plan, then anything can spoil your well-intended international sojourn. If you are clear from the start, you will be blessed to avoid any financial entrapments. Not many people are lucky enough or blessed to start their sojourn with clarity and mental protection.

That's why people like you and me create platforms to share wisdom with others who are about to be trapped, or they are already trapped in some form of cash quandary. If your purpose and plan was to make some good cash within a specific period, the shiny things can lure you out of that plan, so you need to be careful. It is okay to look to others as if you are clueless about the joys of life, or what you are doing, or like your status does not really tie into your position. Always be reminded that you are not living your life for your colleagues or your neighbors, it's you and your family, or you alone if single. You know your purpose and vision. So, stay lit and focused. People may not know why you left home, but you do.

Whether your suit and clothes don't look the part, honestly if you have no one chasing your money and your bank account is loaded, keep the faith and stay on course. You are far richer than many people who look the part but don't have anything to show for their loads of years overseas. If you are trapped, don't feel bad. We are here to break the chains of financial captivity and to ensure you don't keep on sliding into debt through the understanding of the simple and comic tenets shared in this book.

It is possible to look polished without breaking the bank; look sharp. Only that there is a way to look sharp without causing headache. If you meet me, you will know I don't play small *(for laughs on a bright sunny day!)*. I have just mastered the art of getting good and durable stuff from affordable locations. The life of debt taught me wisdom in keeping money. Any town or city should have some outlet stores, cheaper markets, etc. where you can live happily ever after. You just need to be open to people. Ask openly how you can get to these outlets and cheaper markets. Don't pretend. I have seen average expats buying branded perfumes at US$150 in a shop that has its outlet store just a few hundred meters away, and they could easily get the same perfume on sale at US$50 or less!

Before you make a key decision, always bounce it against your vision; if you are honest with yourself, you will easily prevent many of the money wasting decisions. The focused guiding system removes the tendencies of impulse buying to the point that when you see something that could have easily pulled you down a few months back, you will be surprised with the sense of discipline that tells you "wait!"

The power of restraint ensures that you quickly move into your financial freedom and that of the next generation. Most of us have a background where our parents may not have been financially sorted and we are the generation that is trying to break that barrier of financial stagnation and for posterity. Hence, we can't be wasting the entire vision on temporary aggrandizement because you want to look the part. Don't merely look the part. Better be the part. This is very important.

Think about it. If this big luxurious car that you own is depleting your bank account in savings. Take it out. Especially if you are in debt, we will talk about how to escape the trap later. Maybe you need to change your rented house. Move to a cheaper house. Of course, we will talk about it, but if this is the only chapter you will read in this book before you get tired and angry with me, get rid of the things that are unnecessarily draining your accounts! We are talking about financial freedom here; literally disentangling yourself from the chains of captivity. Whether it's an image issue, or merely the debt factor, anxiety, depression, caused by all these manner of issues, don't just be talking about it. Act on it.

There are lots of things such as an education plan and others, which need you to apply your brain. Don't just fall into something because someone else is doing it; for example, enrolling into a master's program because my friend has done it, or someone's wife has done it. Remember your own purpose and plan. If your plan does not require getting a master's degree or PhD now, then reason within yourself and master all the patience to bring the impulse down. Of course, there are instances where God may be directing you towards a path you never thought about, and He may use people to show you such a way. But I believe that God can also make things clear to you, and it is easy to screen a matter whether be it from a deceitful heart or a sincere place of destiny. You know education can be expensive at times, especially if you are not cash-liquid and you have to pay the bills yourself. At least try pushing yourself to secure a scholarship rather than dwindling your little financial resources if possible.

I know that *all achievement comes from a man's envy of his neighbor* as coined by the wise man, Solomon, the former king of Israel; but as long as it concerns us, let us choose to be inspired by things that align with our life goals lest we follow others to their goals, and 20 years down the line get to realize that we left our goals unattended.

We need to continue being inspired by people, but do not drive our spending habits or personal plans based on what someone has done. Be inspired, but take that inspiration and bring it into your own vision; how does it fit in? You may end up doing a global executive MBA, but not now. Say, you have lots of debt - you may need to clear that first. Then later, once you have grown your bank account, you can do more with the available liquidity. This could be the best time to start doing your MBA. Do not rush yourself into avoidable headaches. These are modest lessons you must learn through experience. Although some people say experience is the best teacher, if it causes damage, I would rather learn through counsel to avoid wasting my time.

If you are currently driving a tiny car, it is fine in this season. I have lived this life many times. When the blessing of a bigger car arrives, you will not even be confused. You will jump into that machine without even crying over your lost cash. You will have a better financial foundation to support your proclivities and to protect you from financial frustrations.

It may be painful getting into a smaller house or driving a small car, especially when most of your colleagues and friends 'drive well'; don't worry. Image is always better preserved when *'you are the part, and not when you are trying hard to look the part'*. Most of the people you try to impress now will never even remember your name in the next 10 years. But *'you'* will always be with you. Preserve your future dignity by making wise decisions today.

By buying or *borrowing* this book, I would presume you want to learn something on getting out of debt, or avoiding debt and getting free. I am happy to be of help; but you can do yourself more justice by reincarnating from being the lover of shiny things into a modest but visionary self. Keep the audacious goals alive but do not drown in pretension. Especially in expat-loaded environments; we don't really know each other in these places – and most of the cities are simply melting pots of cultures and passions. You can't even try to impress the citizens of the land because, frankly, they own the land, and one day you would have to leave and go back home if you don't intend to get a permanent residence. By any means, expats in gulf countries don't dream of permanent residence anyways. You must be like a very gifted athlete, military personality, or big-time investor to secure your gulf paradise – otherwise it's always *masalama'a* (*bye or 'good times ahead' in Arabic*) after your tenure in the Middle East. This happens to almost every expat in the region; so, you better leave the place with some money to either jump-start your career back home – in a different country – or indeed to invest and start your own enterprise!

Not all that glitters is gold. Many of the shiny things are only traps placed in your 'freedom path' to mess up your bank account balance. Stay awake!

#don'tleaveyourmoneybehind

Your 'Why'

"Every journey has a reason"

5

Chapter 5: Remember Why You Left

It's crucial to remind yourself **why you left** your home country to seek a foreign job, project, or business opportunity in the first place. Sometimes we tend to forget this fundamental aspect. Maybe you chose to leave because of the money - entailing that the multiplier effect of choosing the overseas opportunity over pursuing a career back home was obvious. Or probably you saw a greater opportunity to grab unique knowledge and competencies, and to accumulate funds which can propel your personal projects and business opportunities, or probably settle some debt or mortgage over your home.

Some of us were compelled by the possibility of speeding up some marriage preparations and setting up a family home. Irrespective of the rationale, everyone has unique reasons why they left home.

There is also another tangent on **how you left**. Did you leave in a very happy, decisive, and passionate mood; or were you hard-pressed and confronted by life pressures that caused you to bid farewell to the land you hold so dearly? Did you embark on a treasure hunt for financial freedom beyond the seas?

Whatever it is for you, there is always a 'why' and a 'how' you left. These two tangents define the crucible of your existence in the current location; and as long as you keep on reminding yourself of these facets, your responses have a way of helping you navigate both the rough and the quite waters. It cements your objectivity and purpose that drives your passion.

If you know that you left to get money as quick as possible and to settle some debts; or you could not establish your first business due to lack of capital (and the home economy could not sustain your dreams) – banks and venture capitalists could not buy into your dream; you have unique propositions of which only you understand the immense potential of your ideas. The way you will view money will be completely different to someone who has no reference point.

One thing I've come to consider as powerful is your ability to repeatedly relive your experience before you left home. Allow all the available emotions to drive you. You can't rely on other people's "whys". There are people who are already financially sorted back home, and probably having a heavy inheritance handed down by their parents. You cannot risk your future by being driven by people who have a completely different agenda for coming overseas. Do not find yourself working on someone's agenda. Create your own game and focus on it.

If your overseas agenda resonates with the theme of this book, it will be wise if you attach yourself to people who are similarly busy building that 'wealth bundle'. People who will keep you focused on the goal and hold you accountable to the core purpose.

If you wrongly attach yourself to people who are not out there for savings & investments, but rather for experiences, you may find yourself going on spending sprees which you will live to regret later.

The Power of Why

Why you left is a very powerful starting point. The response to this question has saved lives, found people ideal spouses, bred patience in people's hearts to wait for a breakthrough regardless of surrounding circumstances, opposition, or persuasion. This is the most powerful nucleus that we all need to sustain the course of what we intend to do during, or after, an international move. Simply by spending some quality time to define your 'why', I can guarantee that you will get an unshakeable compass which will drive your every decision going forward.

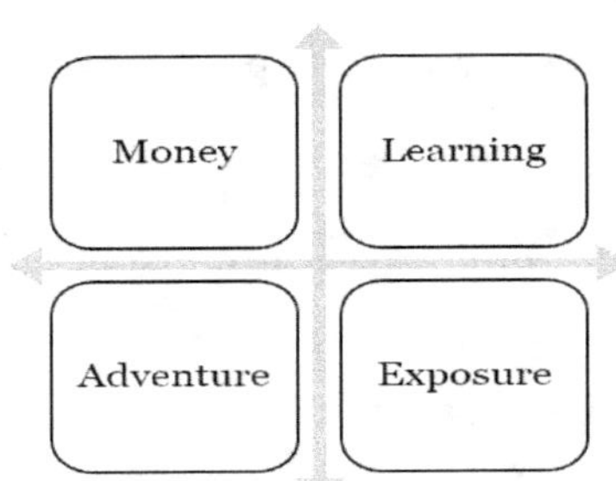

CHAPTER 5

Finding Your Why

Let's assume when you left home you weren't really planning to achieve a specific target. In your very peaceful life, someone just bumped into you, or you stumbled into the current overseas opportunity. You didn't even have an ounce of ideas to move beyond your national borders. How then can you define your why? Let's go back to the moment you accepted the opportunity. So, you stumbled on the opportunity, or it was just cast into your lap. You woke up and it was here in front of you. How did you respond?

What made you say yes? How did you analyze the opportunity? What made you quit your current job or business, or leave your family and friends, to accept this move? That moment of leaving and accepting has somewhere (in between), YOUR WHY. So probably you might have accepted the opportunity because you thought you could get more experience and money - or it was simply an adventure and you believed you would lose nothing by trusting your instincts.

So, for you, did you get persuaded because you felt you would get better experience working away from home, or was it the money; or maybe a possibility of marrying someone from a far-off land? Something like those old fairytales? Was it about changing the legacy of your family and breaking the poverty trap? Was it something to do with learning and creating your own world-class consulting or manufacturing firm back home?

Sometimes it's as simple as getting into a progressive economy where you can learn new concepts that would make you a thought leader in your field when you decide to go back home. Any of these thoughts would have formed your 'why'.

It's not possible that you completely didn't have a reason to leave home. Even in subtle ways, the 'why' was hidden within your unsure response. Whatever the circumstances of your decision, you are here now, and somehow you got whisked to a far-off land and now you are part of your diaspora community. Life has amazing ways of making something out of simple occurrences.

Let's say, for example, your original 'why' was to get international experience or exposure in some specialty – how many years have you been away from home now? Would you say you have managed to justify your 'why'? Have you gained the international experience that you planned to utilise back home? What efforts are you making to gain more experience, or is it just about the company you are working with – or the entire industry eco-system or the massive talent that you have met in your current placement? Are you ready to go back home and make the aspired difference or are you already achieving 'abnormal' growth levels in your current location (*or exponential levels, in better English?*). What about the money? If your main purpose was to make some good money – what intentional decisions have you made to place yourself in a position to gain more money? How many years have you worked in the diaspora; what about the learning and career progress; how many companies have you worked with; what about the progressive salary packages – do you see a significant change in your earning capacity? Is your purpose of making more money being lived and attained? If your core aim was to make money and possibly to go home and do something spectacular, you wouldn't claim that you have now settled because you found a good company, or a good boss, among all the other reasons or excuses you may want to give. Have you made the money? If not, why? If given more time, do you think your habits will be any different to allow you to make the money and still achieve your dreams within the next 5 or 10 years? Or do you still need another 20 years overseas?

These are questions that I didn't ask myself early on in my sojourn to the Middle East. I wish I had a ready-made template way back in 2010 which could keep me sane and intentional in all the decisions that I've made since that time. Initially, I had a clear plan to work in the Middle East for **only 3 years** and make some good cash before returning home. Alas! Life has it and I only woke up from my long slumber after **12 years**!

After the miraculous 12, I realized you can indeed become anything if you didn't plan on becoming something. The focus was money, but I ended up being perpetually broke and constantly struggling to make ends meet in the foreign lands. In hindsight, a career or business back home would have yielded me more returns than working in the Middle East (*money-wise)*. I know that I have possibly gained more professional knowledge, insights, and more exposure from progressive nations, but on the money-side-of-life it has been a journey of frustrated dreams and expectations.

There are some sacrifices that you make without counting the full opportunity costs; or simply having a minimum understanding how life overseas may cost you decades in-between. A simple fact that you may barely get time to work on your own dreams (in most of the foreign lands), or the realities that you may not be able to pay someone to help you around the home, and you have to spend most of your precious time cleaning the house, taking care of the kids, and pretty much satisfying all housekeeping needs; these are realities that may cost you years of personal investments and sweat equity. For most of the expats, back home we would have the luxury of time to explore as many opportunities as possible with the same seemingly little money that you would be paid on the local scene.

The same salary packages that look shiny when leaving home are the same shells that get melted in the foreign land through exorbitant house rentals, children's school fees, motor vehicle costs, house help charges, possible expensive household and clothing items, and then some bank charges if you happen to transgress from the way of financial wisdom.

That's why after breaking-through some tough walls in my own life I found it commendable to spend time on this book with the hope that someone may avoid my type of mistakes, just like many other expats would tell you, and curve a path of true prosperity and financial success.

You may work for a great company, but if they are not paying you well, or what you deserve, then it's a useless venture. If your why was about getting practical experience and you start compromising the learning for some good salary, then you might have lost the way, unless you can define the new experience as a 'revised goal'. In that case, the purpose of learning dwindles – probably you came for the money – that becomes your new why. You might as well pursue both learning and money because the money can also act as a medium to pay-you-through some advance study programs in the overseas location.

It is okay to evolve the why overtime; however, what matters is whether you indeed know your why *(new, old, or revised)*. Do you?

My why has also evolved over time. Now I want massive grounding in the consulting and thought leadership space, plus making exponential strides in savings and investments. Life should not be complicated. Be flexible, but don't lose your core objectives.

It is a sad situation to go back home empty-handed after so many years of being in the diaspora. You may be going back home with a loaded brain. Nevertheless, tangible financial success brings much honor. We can't afford to head back home with many stories and explanations on how life has been unfair and why 'it is tough to work out there'. We can save ourselves from the shame and chaos by being prepared, by conducting some re-configurations of our why and start to re- invent ourselves today. ***This life of looking polished and sharp outwardly, without having any depth of financial freedom is deceptive.***

Money has always been a defense, and so far, it remains the only medium through which real trade is conducted. Whether it comes in notes, coins, or crypto currencies, as long as you have it, you can transact on the surface of the earth and get some really good stuff with it, including your ability to change the world through personal influence, helping the needy, influencing national and industry policies, and creating iconic investments for you, your family, and the entire posterity.

Even if you dare forget everything, never forget why you left home.

#don'tleaveyourmoneybehind

Understanding Debt

"You can't beat what you don't know"

6

Chapter 6: Don't Dare Debt

Understanding Debt

Debt is a weapon of mass (value) destruction. Whether it comes in the form of a mortgage, car loan, personal loan, credit card, overdraft, soft/fast cash—it doesn't matter. By the end of the day, you still owe the lender, and it is not free lunch. In addition, every *'perfect'* loan comes with a penalty. In the corporate world we call this penalty *interest*.

I understand that clever minds have worked hard to devise the two terms 'good' and 'bad' debt. I think it is wrong to ascribe *acceptable* adjectives to debt; we just help people to justify some of their irrational behaviours by quickly choosing to side with *'good debt' (with a big smile)*. And others will quickly justify that a mortgage is the only way to build or buy a home; or the fact that debt is good for scaling up your business, plus all the wonderful meditation tricks that we teach our brains to embrace our strange decisions. Anyways, this is beyond me.

Also be weary of 'investment loans' that deceitfully come in the form of goodwill but with a cunning purpose to sabotage your dreams and destiny. This world can be wicked; don't trust everything you see; and learn not to get excited about everything that looks good. Have you ever heard the adage *'wolves in sheep skins'*?

Now, talking from experience, for personal and accessory loans it is crucial not to exert unnecessary pressure on ourselves for the sake of immediate gratification, or merely to satisfy our desire to have everything shiny when we have not worked the ground. Personal debt usually comes from a place of unquenchable desire and impatience. It is okay to desire good things, but we need to train our minds in the art of patience. Over time, we will realize that we were chasing things that would have come with time, anyway. So, chill. Don't burn your fingers just because you want the latest model of everything. Dream big, but don't force your dream into life – don't forcefully bless yourself.

One of the most powerful writings I am glad to have stumbled upon states; "*but godliness with contentment is great gain. For we brought nothing into the world, and we can take nothing out of it. But if we have food and clothing, we will be content with that. Those who want to get rich fall into temptation and a trap and into many foolish and harmful desires that plunge people into ruin and destruction. For the love of money is a root of all kinds of evil". (1 Timothy 6:6-11 NIV)*

Can Debt be Good?

I may have a contrary opinion to yours but let me say some good things about debt. Observe that I did not say, "things about good debt"!

As an Accounting Fellow, I know that banks are run by good people who have very kind and good intentions. Banks, especially investment banks, small business financiers, or building societies, have a core mandate to support entrepreneurs and the wider society to achieve a decent life and successful businesses. However, these institutions extend their financial support at a profit. This entails that anyone planning to get funding for a business or housing project needs to be wiser to get out of the specific deal being helped, and not bound and frustrated. Therefore, it is commendable to get a corporate loan for a 'somehow' already profitable business for scaling purposes, or for a property with sure revenues that can cover your loans and future interest obligations.

I have heard people say, "I could only manage to build this house because of the loan"; which is true and coming from a sincere heart (of a proud bank customer). Nevertheless, we still need to do the math. *I love talking in numbers.*

For example, if you took a USD100,000 (20-years) loan at 8.0% to buy land and build your home, assuming no down payment "DP" (although banks usually need 15-30% DP) – you will be paying an estimated monthly interest of around USD836 for 240 months (12 months x 20 years), and ultimately you will cough to the bank approximately USD200,000, including an estimated USD100,000 in interest alone. Thus, you can notice that the expected interest is equal to your principal amount *(i.e., the original loan amount has doubled).* Alsc take note that this calculation is simplistic because the actual mortgage calculations will take into consideration property taxation and insurance, plus an additional insurance percentage for the outstanding loan amount. This calculation also excludes your own ongoing maintenance costs, insurance, and city rates.

If you opt to spread the loan to 30 years, the interest portion would become more than the principal amount. Therefore, even if you rent out the house it may not pay back the loan plus financing in 10 years or more. However, if your property is valuable, the fair market value, in the event you decide to sell the property, may be much higher than your mortgage. But this needs proper asset valuation and experienced real estate agents to save the day.

In the above scenario, I am using a layman's approach but coming from years of accounting, auditing, financial advisory, and lots of personal mistakes. The above simple view presents to you what debt can do when you close your eyes to the *cousins* called *haste and interest*. Otherwise, with wisdom, wealth creation is possible.

The best example of a good decision has been witnessed from expats who quickly opt to buy property in their resident countries. Instead of leasing an apartment, they get a mortgage over the apartment and live in their *own* house. I am aware that in principle the house really belongs to the bank until the mortgage is paid off; but for this purpose and understanding I hope you know what I am talking about. Hence, instead of paying rentals to the landlord, the monthly payments go towards settling the bank mortgage. This decision usually works where the expat has a permanent role in their company or project, and they have also done adequate risk assessment to determine the stability of their role in the foreseeable future, say 5 to 10 years. You can also garner confidence if you have multiple income sources that can support the mortgage settlement in case of employment related emergencies.

Instead of paying US$3,000 monthly rentals, you would pay this amount to the bank for the next 10 years, allowing you to purchase a reasonable apartment covering both the principal loan and interest.

That said, whether you want to buy or lease an apartment, it all boils down to what you truly desire as an individual or family. Some people don't just want to take the risk of tying themselves to a mortgage in a foreign land. Sometimes it's an issue of a 'temporary mindset' where you don't want to stay long in one country; and sometimes the banks themselves make it impossible for expats to get sufficient funds to finance a home. Some countries, for example in the GCC, property prices are very high to the extent that, either the bank would cap the loans to be availed by expats, or they would demand a significant percentage of the property value to be covered by the customer. Other considerations include your age at the time of loan repayment. Let's say if you are aged 45 at the time of availing a 20-year mortgage, if the bank's customer age cap is 60 years, your repayment has to be squeezed to 15 years; otherwise, you will straightaway not qualify for the loan. These conditions vary from bank to bank, and they are usually published on the banks' main sites. It is always commendable to educate yourself in these matters and seek guidance from people who have gone the path you want to take.

For expats planning to buy land and build a family home in their motherland, it is important to conduct adequate research that will allow you to understand the latest market dynamics back home. After going through a personal experience of building our own home, I would recommend asking yourself the following questions, and use the answers to devise a formidable home construction plan:

- What is your initial home construction budget?
- What's the desired size of your family home?
- Do you want to build within the city or out in the country (i.e. in a rural area)?
- Do you already have a piece of land, or will you be searching and getting one now?
- Do you have preferred locations based on the distance to your work, business, public services, or schools?
- Do you plan to hire a design and construction company, or do you have a private architect, quantity surveyor, and foreman to do the work for you?
- Do you have preferences in terms of where you will be getting your construction materials, whether locally or imported? Do you have any suppliers in mind?

- Do you have ready cash for the project, or will you be pumping in cash from your monthly salary?

- Would you complement your funds with a bank loan?

After going through these questions, I would recommend that you get clear on the land first, because the presence of the land will form the baseline for most of the decisions. I would also recommend that you devise a holistic construction budget by getting an experienced quantity surveyor to develop a comprehensive bill of quantities (BOQ) which stipulates all the elements, materials and costs required to complete your project. Once you have the numbers you will be able to know exactly how much money you will be able to personally pump into the project over the given period, plus how much you believe should come from other financiers, e.g., banks. The lack of a solid construction budget can lead to frustrations and numerous financial surprises along the way.

Even in cases where you don't have ready cash from the onset of the project, the project budget still helps you to know how long it will take you to finish the project based on the current (staggered) financial sources. You can build on a piece-meal basis, one day at a time. Some people take 5 to 10 years just working on one home project. I believe there is no one-size-fits-all to these things. As long as you have your vision set, just get busy and build (or get) yourself a home!

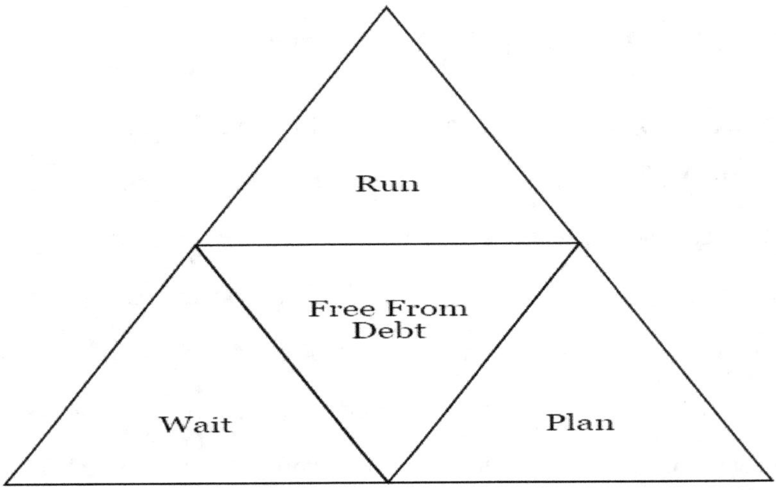

But What About Credit Cards?

Investopedia defines *a credit card as a thin rectangular piece of plastic or metal issued by a bank or financial services company, that allows cardholders to borrow funds with which to pay for goods and services with merchants that accept cards for payment. Credit cards impose the condition that cardholders pay back the borrowed money, plus any applicable interest, as well as any additional agreed-upon charges, either in full by the billing date or over time.*

Different banks have varying conditions on their credit cards and it is always wise to ask and understand such conditions, for example, the interest rates – and whether such rates are calculated and accrued on a daily or monthly basis. In general, it is expected from the bank to offer grace period on credit card loan repayments, and interest is billed only when the customer breaches the grace period. That's why good financial advisors recommend timely settlement of your credit card loans at least clearing 100% of the loan monthly. This is where the main struggle lies for many expats. Credit card loans stay on the personal liability statement for years!

Credit cards are the easiest and fastest route for banks *to enter your life* with tantalizing offers. On a minimum, credit cards look attractive with regard to seamless online payments, travel, retail swipes and for some people, air miles! I will confess that I have ever benefited from the air miles; but the rationale of using a credit card for the sake of getting air miles still beats me! Dave Ramsey, the American personal finance personality, radio show host, author, and businessman, made a good point when he said he's never heard any millionaire saying they made their wealth from credit card points. This was a good one!

You take a credit card with a US$20,000 limit to earn default 100,000 miles that allow you to buy a US$100 wristwatch; if you 'max' the credit through lots of shadowy purchases you can earn around 700,000 air miles, which would in turn allow you to purchase a US$700 air ticket or some fancy jewelry. The flip side? You get stuck with credit card debt for over 3 years still trying to find the edges of the monthly salary. For some expats, the only way to clear credit card debt is when they get their gratuity after leaving a job *(or sadly after being let go from the job).*

The huge downside is that if you consistently fail to make the monthly minimum payments and interest, you end up losing a big chunk of your money to the bank.

My duty is not to discuss the different types of credit cards. However, there is one thing you need to remember, regardless of their types or kinds, all credit cards come from the same family. They all induce avoidable loans, and they have the ability of making you spend the maximum of their allocated limits. Hence, whether your card has a cash back facility (this is where the bank pays you back a small percentage from your accumulated purchases), or whether you get air miles, the perceived personal benefit will never outweigh the bank's profit over your ignorance and spending appetites.

Quoting Davie Ramsey's financial publication, 'Your Top Credit Card Debt Questions Answered', *"There's no positive side to credit card use. There's no beating the system, because it's all been set up to benefit the credit card companies, not you. These companies know you're likely to overspend and rack up thousands of dollars of credit card debt. Over the years, that means you'll pay them thousands of dollars in interest as you carry a balance".* - https://www.ramseysolutions.com/debt/the-truth-about-credit-card-debt.

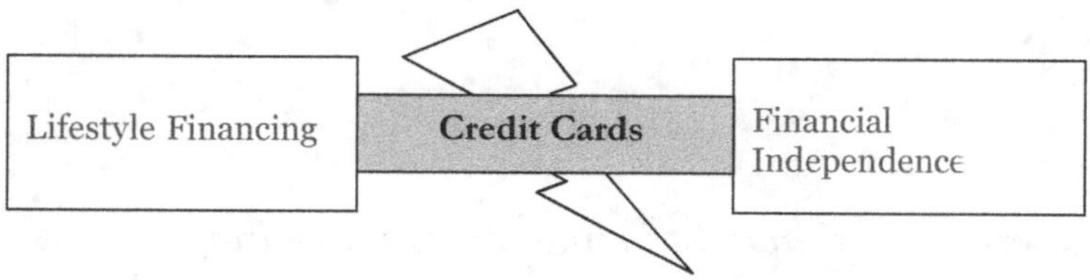

Getting engrossed in debt is like placing fire in your lap. If you are trapped, try all possibilities (within your mental faculties) to get loose. Once free, muster all your strength to never fall into this trap again!

#don’tleaveyourmoneybehind

Getting Free from Debt

"Capturing the fundamentals that allow for freedom"

7

Chapter 7: How to Get Out of Debt

This is a subject I am passionate about; it's something that I have personally experienced, and I have something to say about. I know that in a digital global environment where information sharing is simplified, we all have something to say, right? But the question is, do we really have something to say? So, what I have learnt overtime is that God will take you through experiences that become part of you. Those experiences make you, and when you are given a platform, you are able to share them in depth with people that can relate.

My Story

If you asked me a few years back about money, finance management, or debt issues, I would not be able to share anything tangible. But after having worked for over 12 years on the international scene, away from home, and after making some mistakes on the way, I have – as I said in the preface – gained tons of wisdom. If I had the knowledge I have today I would have lived a better life and made better financial plans and would be obviously wealthier than I am today – but this experience has built me. Now I know better what a dollar means, what a salary is all about and what it can do; how to fearfully receive a salary, to save, disburse, spend, and keep some! I will tell you my modest background.

When I left home in 2010 to join the Big 4 Audit Firm Deloitte in Yemen, I had almost tripled my compensation package; and this happened at a time I had just gotten engaged to my lovely wife, planning to get married within a year. So, when the international move happened, pretty much for the entire period between 2010 and 2011, we were busy working and preparing for the wedding. This meant every amount 'melting' into my bank account essentially had to be channeled to the most important agenda of the age. There wasn't really time to think about financial plans apart from 'the plan'. It's like there was a crucial demand on the bank account. Everything I did was moving towards the big day. We had to save and pay everything to our wedding organizers and ancillary services, including the venue, videography, photographers, the cake, the food, clothes, the ambience, plus all the other niceties. Everything had to be perfect.

The whole excitement of a higher overseas package ended up in the wedding agenda, which me and my wife still consider to be the most beautiful thing to happen in our youth.

After the wedding was sealed, life was good, but there was life happening as we reminisced of the miracle we were witnessing for the first time – marriage. Then the eventful ‘Arab Spring’ happened. The unprecedented protests started in Tunisia, precisely on 17th December 2010, when a Tunisian street vendor, Mohammed Bouazizi, set himself on fire to protest the arbitrary seizing of his vegetable stand by police over failure to obtain a permit. History references indicate that the ‘uprising’ affected several countries including Tunisia, Morocco, Syria, Libya, Egypt, Yemen, and Bahrain. In Yemen, the anti-government protest in the Capital Sana’a started on 3rd February 2011. And this meant the new couple had to figure out how to survive and raise a family within the reality of an unpredictable environment.

We didn’t have much time as the escalation of the uprising was imminent. We had to think fast. The wise thing was to start applying for jobs in other countries. As grace had it, God opened a new door for us to move to Bahrain where I joined another Big 4 Audit Firm KPMG, and I worked for the firm for around 4 years. However, some interesting decisions (looking back) were made at the beginning of this new journey. I caught up with the time when my eyes were opened and I perceived that I had landed in a different terrain of the Middle East – a place where loans are cheaper, and banks chase you without any tangible collateral apart from your committed monthly salary (*where they can chop your money before you even see the monthly salary text message*). For any new employee, the banks only care if your monthly salary is set on a specific minimum amount, and you automatically qualify for anything amazing, from credit cards, overdrafts, personal loans, automobile loans, and you can even get a mortgage people! So, I was somehow 'lucky' to be among the elite group that qualified for everything. I said, okay, at least we can start working on some property project back home; and I thought of getting a small machine that can drive us from point A to point B with no hassles. A secondhand car could do the magic. The banks did a miracle of sorting that out as well. And of course, we needed to have a credit card *(not for easy money)* but for online payments, ease-of-travel and all the wonderful justifications that made sense then. But the hidden reality was that there was a dent of debt on my bank account; a hybrid of good and bad debt which meant 'bad debt' anyways.

That debt wasn't an easy thing. Life was happening, and our family somehow started growing. We started having children. Then I realized, ooh man! Kids need money, and our career choices had to be tweaked as well to suit the evolving terrain.

I know this may sound normal to many expats because this is pretty much a standard picture of many expat homes across the globe – one spouse working (mostly the man), single income source, 'mama' takes care of the kids plus the home, and acts as *the minister of interior and chairman of foreign affairs.* And the custom family owns lots of stuff commonly obtained through bank loans and credit cards.

For us, at this stage we had to figure out how to survive and make sure we take care of our baby. This meant changing our spending habits, although we didn't really have any bad habits. We just had to try to see if we could still tweak the already tweaked lifestyle. Unfortunately, demands were on the rise versus the company's compensation policies. Many of you can relate. Companies don't simply change compensation policies just because someone is misbehaving with the banks *or contributing to the nation's population growth agenda.*

Available options were to dig a little deeper into the credit card, and then to activate the overdraft facility to help the survival agenda. Does this sound familiar? And rationale was all around us – the baby needed some food, diapers, clothes, and recreational stuff. We made sure the baby boy remained warm and cuddly, and happy. And we also needed to float. That's what good parents do.

The debt grew like a shuttle being built for some near-term galactic flight. Then our second child came, an amazing cuddly and bright daughter. Now we had two kids to take care of – as much as these 'cuties' filled our home with joy, laughter, and thanksgiving to God, there was a reality of double responsibility. For couples who get kids of the same gender, they easily transfer some of the baby clothes and stuff from one blessing to the next. But when you have a boy and then a girl, you can't just dump all the 'blue stuff' to the 'pink-desiring' bundle. So, for us it meant getting lots of other stuff for the daughter – and you can guess how that looked like on the monthly net earnings and the continual struggle of making the bank happy on the other hand.

In 2016, I got a new job opportunity in the State of Qatar which provided the much-needed kick on our net earnings, considering all the prevailing financial issues. And as *some* expats would know, you can't just leave a country without settling local debts; and I had to transfer the existing loan to my new bank in the new location, which meant starting a new job from a *negative financial space*. Now do you see why I qualify to talk on this subject?

Coming to Qatar we had the pressure to fix the carried forward financial baggage whilst working on a property project and other critical matters back home. You don't buy land and leave it empty! This reminds me of the scripture that states, *"Who starts constructing a house without counting the cost, or which king wages war against a mighty army without considering the strength & weaponry of the other army?"* Somehow, for us, being without a plan, we had to build on the jump. We were already on the project – so we needed more loans to fix the project. This was like pouring more and more petrol on the fire. You could see the trajectory – from a simple thing that started in 2012 just to get a piece of land, get a car, and sort out some settling costs, the snowball became a habit and kept on blowing up. I learnt that if you get comfortable with the first loan, the next one does not scare you anymore. For us, it took forever to pay back this accumulated loan.

Having no additional income, it meant the accumulation had to be sorted out only from the salary. But as God would have it, we finally had our first experience of paying-off all debts in 2020! Woohoo! We could hardly believe it. Honestly, it felt like having a new lease of life. One thing we now know is that it is indeed possible to pay off debt; any kind of debt.

I have made it sound easy here but trust me it was not an easy journey. We had to sacrifice a lot in terms of our lifestyle, from entertainment, just being human, and all the other things that people do. There are lots of things that our family could not do (intentionally and unintentionally). Living in the Gulf, you literally need to spend on almost everything; a simple weekend outing easily turns into a shopping spree in this region. Sometimes, due to the beautiful hot desert climate, in summer, outings happen in shopping malls as everyone tries to shop under the air conditioners – and this automatically translates into a fully-fledged family outing. You need to get your meals at the mall, and then do some window shopping, which easily turns into the real thing. So, imagine you are broke and stuck. The best way is to avoid the shopping malls!

That's what we did for a greater part of the debt 'bondage'. Embarrassingly, sometimes we had to turn down family invitations when we realized we would be forced to buy lots of 'eventful' things to satisfy the minimum requirements of such invitations. We are the only ones who knew the reality of our bank accounts, so we just had to humbly say no to anything that took us more and more below the 'poverty line'.

Imagine taking your kids to the park after cooking your own food at home (what we graciously call *an organic picnic*) and you believe the kids will understand the underlying money-saving agenda. Somehow, they open their eyes to the premium playground, joyrides, some ice-cream, and more of the stuff that makes their life cozy. The embarrassment of saying no to each of their requests is also heart-breaking, and the only way to avoid such encounters is, again, staying at home. But what a life! Even just attempting a city ride to detox from the closed home environment, your kids would still see doughnuts and real food on the billboards – and this starts a whole unwelcome conversation in the car. Simple things that become abominations. Again, what a life!

For us, we had to identify the best way to make the kids happy without sugar-coating the circumstances. We also made sure we don't develop a household jargon of poverty and struggle to ensure the kids don't keep that stuff in their innocent but powerful craniums. They joined us in the pay-off-debt agenda. We learnt tons of lessons together.

One of the wisest men to ever grace the face of the earth said, *"A borrower is a slave to the lender"*. The borrower is enslaved, trapped, squeezed, and disabled. It's a painful process. You can't even choose the type of house or car you want. Perhaps you have a choice but it's usually the circumstantial type of choice.

Today, I selectively still finance acquisitions and investments using debt, but I am more careful to leverage the cost of debt on the returns envisaged on such acquisitions and investments.

CHAPTER 7

Practical Lessons on Paying-Off Debt

Believe in the Supernatural

There is a bigger world beyond our planet; and I believe it is important to believe in the supernatural and that miracles are possible and still happen today. When you believe in someone greater and wiser than yourself; when you believe in God, you are not going to be bound by circumstances. For sure, God has a purpose for your life, and we all need to seek His guidance when we are stuck financially. No human wisdom will pull us out of a deep financial mess. No human wisdom. It is of course true that as people we do rely on one another; and it is for the same reason that I wrote this book to share whatever I've leant on this journey so that I can impart practical wisdom to those who care to listen; but to a greater extent, a simple thing like you being able to access this book, it take God's guidance to pull you out of the closet, and to bring you to the counter or online page where you are able to bump into some resonating wisdom. Beyond such guidance, what God does also is to open doors that you cannot open with your own strength, including new job opportunities or a business venture and human connections.

Honestly, for someone who is only relying on a meager monthly salary to clear a mountain of debt, the journey may be too daunting even to simply try. This is where God comes through to open doors of opportunity in your current work environment or elsewhere because He is not limited by location, distance, time, abilities, or economics. You may simply get a promotion and you start getting more money – or you get appointed in unique places where you start global trotting, and you get more responsibilities and connections that increase your monthly earnings. Sometimes, God may literally open a door to an unbelievable job – and you automatically get more money and other benefits. Am not just speaking like your routine motivational speaker. These are things that happened to me and am speaking as a credible witness about the amazing hand of God in my own life.

At some point when I was stuck with a huge debt, God opened a door into a job opportunity where I managed to clear the backlog of debt in less than 6 months. A mountain that should have taken me forever was cleared before the end of the same year I made the move. I know this didn't fully fall within the definition of luck, because this was not the first encounter where I have seen God moving in incredible ways throughout my life.

With the lessons learnt in the past 9 years of paying off debt, we quickly became wiser on how to keep money and carefully disburse some into priority areas. We prioritized squaring off the bank obligations.

I am cognizant that not everyone will be a person of faith; however, we all have a source of confidence and trust. For me, my source is God. I only ask you to hear me from that standpoint of faith. God is a primary refuge in times of trouble and uncertainty. No matter the size of your mountain, when you commit it to God, success is inevitable.

'Count Your Flocks'

By counting your flocks, I mean you need to be open about how much debt you owe the world. Be open about how much debt you owe the world – just saying that again! For us it was the personal loan, the overdraft, the credit cards, and a few more random soft loans from friends. Whew! I am only giving these examples for you – so that when you say that you are in debt – what happens for most people who are stuck, they keep on digging into more and more debt (as long as it looks like debt, they will jump on it for survival). If you are lucky, you may only have one credit card. However, for the average survivor, there is mortgage, automobile loans, overdraft facilities, credit cards (all of them), personal loans, company loans, company advances, borrowings from friends and family (remember everyone, don't forget them – you owe them money). Now aggregate all these loans. This forms your gross debt, and you need to work from this amount - from this mountain.

Now you can look at the aggregate debt against your net salary, not your gross pay, making sure that you have already removed the fixed payments we mentioned earlier. Make sure to remove first the rentals, school fees, home support, mobility, utilities, faith-based payments, and charity, among other fundamentals. Even groceries sometimes are fixed because we can't really reduce consumption, can we? Maybe. For some people this is arguable. Man must eat a minimum amount of food!

And after all this, how much would you realistically be remaining with monthly? And how does the estimated cash balance look like in the face of the aggregate or gross debt *(your real-life Goliath)*?

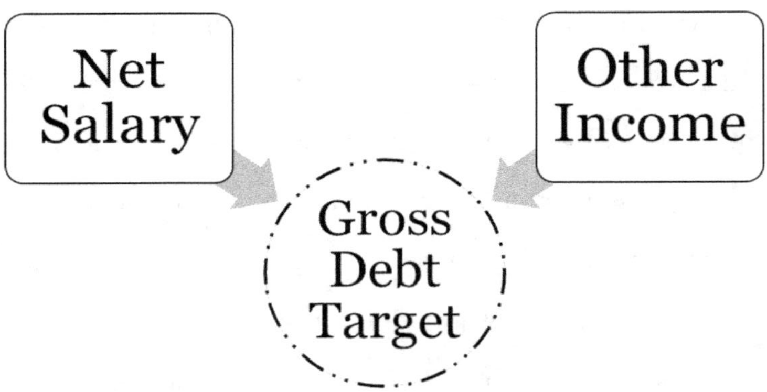

There is a story told about a young boy called David who fought the giant Goliath. Although King Saul offered him the best armor to put on when facing the giant, he told the king that he was not experienced in using sophisticated weaponry. However, he had been a herdsman for a long time, and he had killed a lion and a bear with his hand – and he didn't want to use the strange armor at this time. He trusted in God and took some small 5 stones and put one in his sling and slung it towards an open space on the head of the giant, and the giant came sprawling down with a huge splat. And the giant dies. It's a true story.

This also applies to the debt. When you look at the goliath of your debt versus what you are earning monthly, do not be dismayed – that's why I started with God. God helps you to gain faith and wisdom, so you look at the amount versus the debt – it looks very impossible, usually. But we win from here once we look at the numbers.

You need to break it down. If you need to pay back the debt using the current earnings, for whatever number of years, mortgage may go to 20 or 30 years, school loans would take a varied number of years. Just thinking about it sounds like lifelong imprisonment. I couldn't even breathe for 9 years! But don't worry. We need to break it down.

The problem is not the small stone that needs to bring down the goliath. The issue is in the make-up of the source of the small stone. I hope you get this. You have your monthly pay whether double salary for both spouse or only a single salary from one spouse, you need to look at the gross pay that you are getting, and again re-look at the fixed costs we mentioned above – analyze these costs like a pro. One by one. For example, if you are lucky to receive US$10,000 and your house rent is US$4,000, there is no wisdom, right? Like why are you paying 40% of your gross earnings towards a temporary housing solution? This doesn't make sense. So, you automatically know that this is a low hanging fruit. I know your faith may be larger than most of us, but I am just trying to talk you into combined practical experience on money matters. I believe even God expects us to be good stewards of every blessing that comes our way. On the surface, 40% rentals don't look like a smart move to me.

If your desire is to pay off debt, don't just spend more time in prayer but also apply the knowledge that you are getting from credible sources, including this book. This is called wisdom. Ask yourself why you are paying your hard-earned money into all these so-called fixed costs? Who fixed them anyway?!

It's better to reduce these costs even if it looks like you are debasing yourself and becoming a target of societal shame, by going somewhere smaller but smarter. The joy of your strange decision will be massive savings!

If you are the one paying for your children's school fees, is there anything you can do about the committed monthly or term-based payments? Obviously, every parent looks out for the best for their kids unless you are one of those uncommon run-away humans. However, you still need to wisely consider the current school you are sending your kids contemplating whether it's unreasonably draining your bank accounts. Moreover, what about the available alternatives where your kids would get equal or competitive education without you breaking the bank? Good to think about it.

The other interesting component is food. As simple as this may sound, most of us love to make impulse food purchases when we seem to have the cash (usually around the month end) or when we visit shops under the banner of hunger. But if your food budget is another US$2,000 for example, do you really need to spend all this amount on feeding your family? There are many alternatives when it comes to reducing the food and groceries budget. Whether you choose to target promotions, clearances, or traditional markets, it is better than living under the façade of well-to-do-people.

Let us be honest, whether you get your chicken from the most sophisticated hypermarket or a stall along the street on your way home, the end of the transaction will still look like a sizzling chicken on the same ceramic plates. Most of the time there is nothing special in the chicken except for the sentimental value of interfacing with people who have already made it in life. However, this book is not about feelings or emotional benefits. We are focusing on how to get out of debt so that we can later comfortably go to those expensive hypermarkets, and not just to get a chicken, but a whole turkey wrapped in banana leaves and sprinkled with mushrooms. A whole large life experience!

Whatever you buy and eat, can we consider other sources like planting your own garden for the vegetables in your backyard or some small plastic bags and buckets on your balcony or in the kitchen. I am cautious not to make strange propositions to people who cannot understand my language. But I believe most expats know what I am talking about. Very few people can afford massive villas possessing flamboyant backyards and gardens. Most expats somehow survive in unusual spaces. It's part of the journey to the Promised Land. We need to find convenient ways of doing stuff until we have gone past the season.

Sometimes all it takes is talking to the right people to tell you about the local vegetable & fruits, fish, and meat markets; and you will be amazed at the competitive bargains you will get for your weekly food budgets. And when it comes to confectionery, can you blend between home baking and convenient shopping?

What about entertainment and family outings? Do you love eating out? You can easily cut down on that behavior. For example, if you were spending US$1,000 for entertainment, when you are paying back debt it's not entertainment time. Of course, you don't depress yourself just for the world to feel sorry for you and to attract people's sympathy. Don't be extreme. It's possible to enjoy your life as you pay back debt, but you need to make sure that the unnecessary chaff is cut out from the equation. You can go out with your family once a month and that's fine. For the rest of the weeks, you can buy nice food and barbeque at home. You can also have nice small family gatherings for the kids to enjoy and for the adults to talk sense towards a solid future.

It is 'paying-back-debt time'. You can't keep on copying other people's lifestyles. Focus on your mission and sort out your life. No time for strange comparisons.

Family Support and Helping the Needy

For most expats, especially those of us coming from developing countries, it is not strange to have dependent parents and extended families who rely on your monthly paycheck. It could be siblings, or first-degree relatives; but in some cultures, the line goes all the way to the fifth degree – some of them you've never met except for some miraculous meeting on Facebook and life happens from there. Some of them will be like *"I am a distant cousin of your father"*. When you crosscheck with your mum, she gladly confirms that yes, this cousin is your own blood! One more addition to the list of dependents!

According to the World Migration Report 2020 by the United Nations' International Organization for Migration (IOM), International remittances increased to USD 689 billion in 2018, the top 3 remittance recipients being India (USD 78.6 billion), China (USD 67.4 billion) and Mexico (USD 35.7 billion). The United States remained the top remittance-sending country (USD 68.0 billion) followed by the United Arab Emirates (USD 44.4 billion) and Saudi Arabia (USD 36.1 billion). These figures reconcile so well considering that the majority of global immigrants come from the recipient nations, whilst most of the labor requirements are fulfilled in the remittance nations.

Although the sound (not just the sight) of the above numbers may be unbelievable, each one of us (expats) has a small contribution that makes these remittances possible. For some of us it is all about monthly remittances to support family and friends, or to maintain savings in home bank accounts. For some expats, it is all about making investments back home in real estate, money markets, equity markets, and personal businesses, among so many other things that money can do.

Dilip Ratha, the Lead Economist, Migration and Remittances and Head of KNOMAD wrote on World Bank Blogs, stating, "*In 2021, the top five remittance recipients in current US dollar terms were India, China, Mexico, the Philippines, and the Arab Republic of Egypt. As a share of gross domestic product, the top five remittance recipients in 2021 were smaller economies: Tonga, Lebanon, the Kyrgyz Republic, Tajikistan, and Honduras. The United States was the most significant source country for remittances in 2020, followed by the United Arab Emirates, Saudi Arabia, and Switzerland.*

The cost of sending money across international borders remained high, around 6.4 percent on average in the first quarter of 2021. Sending remittances to Sub-Saharan Africa is particularly high (8 percent). Corridor-specific data reveal that remittance costs tend to be higher when remittances are sent through banks than through digital channels or money transmitters offering cash-to-cash services".

In 2021 the World Bank further reported that remittances to low- and middle-income countries were projected to have grown at a strong 7.3 percent to reach $589 billion in the year. This return to growth is more robust than earlier estimates and follows the resilience of flows in 2020 when remittances declined by only 1.7 percent despite a severe global recession due to COVID-19, according to estimates from the World Bank's Migration and Development Brief. - https://www.worldbank.org/en/news/press-release/2021/11/17/remittance-flows-register-robust-7-3-percent-growth-in-2021.

A significant portion of the above-quoted billions of dollars help to support expats' families back home. The real and ultimate impact on the home economies depends on how the recipient families choose to use that money. If it is only for food, shelter and survival, the expenditure mostly leads to the local retailers' benefit. If they use it to invest in some sort of ventures, there could be a lasting impact on those families assuming they find 'gold' in their quest for financial independence.

I am a big believer in helping people. Beyond charity, I believe our giving should be targeted towards making a lasting impact on people's lives. For example, if you are supporting young people to access education, that is a noble responsibility, and you are doing a great job for posterity. Or if you are providing medical support for your family, this is a big deal.

I am also a big believer in honoring our parents by virtue of their position and role in our lives. It is understandable that there are some people who had what are called absent fathers or mothers. But if they are still alive, I will go with the belief of helping them regardless of what happened in the past. By virtue of DNA and role, they are our biological parents – take care of them and see the blessings that will come your way.

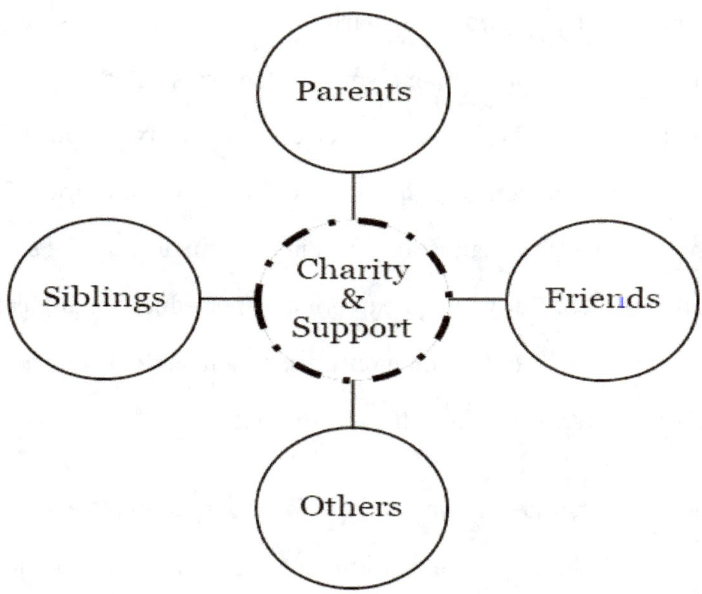

But then remember, we are still paying back debt. The key thing is to consider the amounts you are giving away to support parents, siblings, and strangers, or even for faith-based causes. Also look at the frequencies of the various 'giving's' and the associated rationale. I know this may sound radical but allow me to finish. Don't quit thinking of settling your debts fast just because I am critiquing your 'wonderful' giving adventures.

For example, let's say you are the only one who pays for school fees for one of the lads in your extended family, and you have been doing this for some time now – it means you can't reduce the default academic fees and you can't even stop the charity because no one else will do it for them. This is a commitment you need to trust God to continue supplying finances to allow for such gracious generosity. If you stop the good gesture, your beneficiary may drop out of school and their future reality may come back to haunt you, even in your small corner of success. Not a brilliant idea. But you can explore cheaper educational locations or schools if you believe that the monthly payments are devouring a big chunk of your potential savings. If okay, do that.

Then there are other people who ask you for money simply because they know you will find a way to get the amount, irrespective of whether you take it from the credit card or overdraft. They don't know the implications. Amazingly these will be the cohort who also dress better than you, and they possibly attend all the happening events in town whilst you, the financier, is languishing at home thinking about the next paycheck. This may not be the case for everyone, but the reality is that for most people or even siblings who keep on calling for cash, it's usually because they want to sustain a lifestyle they don't have a foundation for. And why should you be a willing accomplice in helping them live an artificial life?

Always remember you have your own obligations, and if you are married you need to fend and invest for your family as well. I am not saying you should close your ears to the needs of others. However, you need to be honest regarding your capacity to meet certain requests. If you don't have liquid cash in your bank account, it means you don't have money. Don't take debt to support other people's lifestyles. If they are not aged parents or ailing siblings, they can as well take their own debt to support their lifestyle.

Expat life is not as easy as perceived by many. You usually live away from your family and you are constantly chasing personal targets and objectives. You cannot be a financier of someone's luxurious lifestyle. And to avoid the headache, you should stop condoning the casual cash requests – whether from relatives or friends.

To determine authentic needs, don't make emotional decisions. Ask all the necessary questions and then wisely determine the amount you can afford without the impulse or feeling that someone will complain against your giving. Even for your parents, if they truly love you, and care to see you thriving when you go back home, they should appreciate your financial situation as well.

One evil I have seen under the sun is when well-meaning family members and friends keep on squeezing amounts from you, you automatically plateau, and no one really grows beyond the usual mediocre financial capacity. In fact, it is better for your family to allow you some space to grow, so that when you have broken through the family's traditional financial ceiling, you will be able to inspire the rest of the siblings and extended family members to break their own financial roofs as well. Success leaves a trail.

For the above recommendations to make sense, I encourage you to look at the numbers again. Have a sober session of reviewing the amounts you have been giving people each month and spread that across the past 1 year, 2 years, or 5 years. And then compare that to the outstanding debt amounts. I bet you will be shocked! Probably your debt, which is being paid via the usual standard monthly payroll deductions could have been swallowed by a lumpsum settlement of your accumulated savings. For example, if your monthly average financial support is US$1,000, it means your annual support is US$12,000; and if you extend this steady support to 3 years, you would have given US$36,000 over time. If these simple numbers can show you the accumulation-effect, what more the compounding effect of invested earnings? If the annual US$12,000 was invested in the money market for the 3 years, with an additional US$1,000 every month, you could easily have made over US$50,000 within the same period.

Of course, I am not alluding that you should have stopped helping people, but you can use a simulation of, say, reducing the annual support to US$8,000 after getting rid of unjustified support stuff; then you would be investing the redeemed US$2,000 per year, and making around US$170 contributions per month. This would still give you over US$9,000 over the 3 years instead of a zero-sum bank account!

I am trying to open your eyes to the reality that whatever amounts you loosely give away, you are eating from your capacity to quickly move out of debt and start building a healthy savings and investment plan.

Subscriptions

The modern life demands a lot of 'feeders' into our daily routine to make life endurable and livable, and this calls for numerous service subscriptions - from routine mobile phone and home broadband subscriptions to all the wonderful online streaming services. And then there is the tantalizing gym or club memberships. All these services are commendable, especially if you also have an employer or business that covers such budgets for you. But if you are drawing the payments from your paycheck, this is one area you can make massive cost reductions in.

During the 2020-2021 Covid19 pandemic season we witnessed expats who desperately wanted to trade-off their club memberships with cash or other tangible benefits, food, or something they can liquidate quickly to get cash. This season helped many people to identify priorities and to also feel the depressing impact of a negative bank account. Though not to make it a celebrated experience, I believe that most expats will come, and have come, out of the pandemic season wiser and more intentional, especially with regard to financial freedom.

For most people, monthly subscriptions are usually underutilized, and if we truly apply the proportional return on investment, i.e., the value obtained from the monthly payment, we might realize that we have only gained less than 10% of the services. For example, video streaming services – how many shows and movies do you watch during the week? If you have kids, maybe the kids try to maximize the benefits. But are such sessions benefiting their academic progress? Just me musing.

Are all the existing subscriptions something that you really need to have, or are you simply excited to be among the right league, like simply wanting to be 'in the know' when discussing the new reality shows at work? Take out the stuff that you don't need. You may say but I need premium YouTube; that's fine. Keep YouTube for the core purposes, but what about the rest? I also need Netflix – it's not so expensive after all. Okay, maybe keep Netflix. However, all the small monthly payments add up, you need to be wiser to conduct an annual cost assessment and see whether you are still having good rationale for keeping some of these services.

It makes no financial sense to maintain five video streaming subscriptions just because you believe the other services don't have that one series you only watch once a month!

Of course, it is honorable to stay connected, especially in the case of the more justified subscriptions like the mobile phone.. But what mobile packages do you subscribe to? Is it those with lots of add- ons you don't even know what they 'add' to your life? To be honest, maybe I have become more brutal and aggressive with unnecessary spending after the bad experience I have had with debt – but it should be normal for everyone who is trying to gain financial freedom to think in those lines as well. You need to take time to evaluate whether you can justify the amounts going to the mobile services provider. If you mostly use your phone for calling, texting, and accessing the standard applications, make sure to trim the rest of the stuff that you are unnecessarily billed for. Simply, I mean choose a package that satisfies your communication and connectivity needs. That's it. Sounds simple right?

And there are other packages which have variable pay on your data consumption; after you 'burn' the minimum data, for the rest of the weeks before the next billing date the mobile services carrier charges you additional costs, without even thinking about it. That's a waste of money. It is better to opt for packages that keep you connected albeit at slower speeds.

Clothes and Fashion

What about the clothes? Most of our cabinets have things that we don't even touch. Shoes, dresses, shirts, everything. Of course, it's admirable to look well, look sharp, and smell good too. But you don't need to burn all your money on looks alone. There are better ways of getting cheaper but nice stuff. Even if you dress to kill 24/7 whilst having the dragon-type debt in the bank, any artificial praises don't bring you peace.

You can look just as smart by buying nice clothes (that look expensive, durable, and probably branded) from outlets, instead cf chasing every new fashion from the main stores. I have done this several times and I've been amazed at the kind of deals you get at outlets.

The other way is to chase promotional seasons and online store discounts. If you have sufficient time to wait *(if your purchase is not an emergency),* always take time to compare the store and online deals across various brands before making the purchase; especially where you will be spending a reasonably significant amount.

I have also found that buying 'moderately expensive' and good quality shoes and clothes will help you to avoid making repeated purchases for the same items. For men, if you get five decent shirts and four well-fitting and durable suits, plus a Kenneth Cole or Cole Haan shoe, you should be sorted for the next year or two. For women, this could be a rough terrain; however, quality purchases of matching materials would still ensure that you don't routinely buy new stuff for every corporate or family event. For example, you can intentionally purchase materials by colors, from the dress to the bag. This will ensure that for every green or indigo dress, you have an existing matching element in a shoe, bag, or scarf, hence allowing you not to keep on jumping into the next shop every time you get an invitation to events. This behavior demands more intentional living than DNA-induced proclivities. Behaviors can be changed.

The reality about debt is that, whatever happens, you need to pay it back. So even if your lifestyle puts up a façade of success, the bank will always be waiting for that monthly credit to your account. If you delay, even by only a day, it looks like the whole bank is calling and chasing you. Have you ever heard the saying *"there is no peace for the wicked"*? I am not saying that you are wicked when you have debt, but the fear and emotional chaos just feels like you are not far from that definition.

> All debt must finally be paid back

It is understandable that cost reduction in areas like house rental or educational costs may not happen immediately due to existing contracts, regulatory school terms, among other standard issues. But with good planning, it's just one year or a few months before you can make the necessary changes, without disrupting your household and kids' education. You can progressively change the house by proactively starting to look for another house. When you are in debt your drive is to cut costs on everything that has the capacity to take money from your bank account. Unless your company provides actual accommodation or rental allowance, the approach is to find affordable housing to align with the mission of paying off the stubborn debt. The mission is to avoid the persistent zero at the end of the month.

Most people who are in debt, their net account balance a few days after month end is zero. A friend of mine, Tariq, who's been inspired by Robert Kiyosaki always tells me *"This zero is the problem. We need to deal with this zero."* If we can take out all the unnecessary costs, we will end up having more money in the net income equation.

The Eventual Debt Pay-Back

There are multiple approaches, the common ones being the snowball method and the avalanche method. Wells Fargo provides the below succinct explanation:

The "snowball method," simply put, means paying off the smallest of all your loans as quickly as possible. Once that debt is paid, you take the money you were putting toward that payment and roll it onto the next-smallest debt owed. Ideally, this process would continue until all accounts are paid off. As you roll the money used from the smallest balance to the next on your list, the amount "snowballs" and gets larger and larger and the rate of the debt that is reduced is accelerated.

In contrast, the "avalanche method" focuses on paying the loan with the highest interest rate loans first. Similar to the "snowball method," when the higher-interest debt is paid off, you put that money toward the account with the next highest interest rate and so on, until you are done. By focusing on the loans that are the most expensive to carry, in the long run, would effectively mean you should pay less over time with this method, as it addresses high interest first.

You may save some money with the "avalanche method," but if the principal is large, the time it may take to pay off debt with the highest interest can be discouraging and make it difficult to stick to the plan. Paying off small debts quickly can feel rewarding. If you prefer to see progress quickly and work your way up, then the "snowball method" may be a better fit for your debt management goals. - https://www.wellsfargo.com/goals-credit/smarter-credit/manage-your-debt/snowball-vs-avalanche-paydown/.

In our initial debt repayment testimony, we applied the snowball method. We started tackling the overdraft, then the credit card, before pouncing on the personal loan. If you have all, check the smallest one and cut it off! Commit not to use your credit card for routine purchases anymore; and if you must use the card somewhere, make sure you deposit cash into the card before you make such payments, or commit to an almost immediate repayment of whatever amount you used. This will help you avoid growing/digging the debt hole again. This advice is directed at people who are deep in debt and trying to get out of the ditch first. There is separate advice for people who have mastered using credit cards to build points or airmiles that are converted for other purchases and travel. This is a separate topic not fully helpful for someone who's simply trying to breathe.

Another best way to avoid using credit cards is by requesting a Prepaid or Reloadable Debit Card from your bank. This card allows you to add money to your card's balance periodically, which you then can spend as needed. A reloadable debit card, on the other hand, is not linked to a bank account. So, unlike a bank debit card, which normally allows you to spend as much money as you have in the account, a reloadable card limits you to the money you have loaded onto it. - https://www.investopedia.com/reloadable-debit-cards-how-they-work-5078347.

Once you commit to pay off your debt it becomes an exciting adventure – a very exciting experience, to the effect that when you see that 'goliath-of-a-debt' coming down your adrenaline levels just keep on spiking, and you really want to see all entanglements crashed. If the bank told you the loan had a 5-year tenure, you fight to have that burden gone in 2 years! That means 3 years of your life redeemed! This passion needs to resonate around the home with your spouse and kids. And if you have animals around the house, let them get involved. The whole family is on a mission!

You need to commit to this agenda. Have a plan and targeted timeline to ensure there's clarity on the newly adopted direction and be sure to commit to paying off the debt within the specified period. And going back to my reference to God. When you commit to do something admirable like this, your faith is unshakeable, and God himself creates a way for you.

There is something about passion and determination that I can't explain, but I see the evidence all the time. There is something that happens when a person has purposed in his or her heart to change the status quo. It is like the whole universe convenes to support your concrete objectives. This 'something' can only be explained as faith. Until you commit to the debt repayment agenda, there is no faith to support your desire – and all those wishes would only end up as a mere fantasy.

Sometimes all you need to do is to draft the debt repayment plan, regardless of the bleak and impossible picture that it presents. Your salary alone may not be up to the task of demolishing the walls; but what if God is waiting for your plan to open a door that doubles your income? The problem is in not starting at all. If you are serious about paying off the debt you must at least draw the plan!

If there is anything worthy of meditation from this book are the following words:

"Whoever works hard will have plenty to eat, but whoever wastes their time with dreams will always be poor". Proverbs 28:19 (ERV)

Paying-Off Debt Versus Savings

The most common question I get from my contacts is whether one can make debt repayments whilst also building a healthy savings nest or an emergency fund. My response has always been, 'it depends'. Not everyone is financially savvy to understand the implications of splitting their cash between debt repayment and savings. However, it is possible to do simple math and analyze the viability the duo-model through the following questions:

- Is your net income (salary plus other income minus fixed costs) more than sufficient to meet the minimum debt repayments?
- Can the surplus income (after making the minimum debt repayments) be invested in assets that can yield higher interest rates than the financing costs on your existing loans?

If the surplus cannot be invested in profitable short - or medium- term investments, it is pertinent to focus on maximizing your debt settlements by growing your snowball with speed instead of splitting the net income between debt and savings. However, if you are a savvy investor or have strong partners who can invest your funds in high-yielding assets or business ventures, it is also commendable to expand your income streams which would in turn allow you to clear the debt faster.

Another key consideration is to make sure you understand the differences between savings, investments, and emergency fund. Although people opt to live a free-wheeler lifestyle where all their money is dumped into a single bucket, it's critical to understand the differences.

Savings entail the liquid (available) cash which you stash away in a routine debit bank account, or fixed deposit account for growth or future investment plans. This money is readily available and can easily be withdrawn from the bank. The emergency fund is created for 'emergency purposes', mostly to sustain you during a job spell, business failure, or major family crisis. Financial experts recommend growing an emergency fund at the equivalent of your 3 to 9 months' basic pay. Investments are intentional buckets of cash placed in short to long terms investments, such as: money markets, private and public equity investments (purchase of company shares), transactional deals (one-off purchase and sale of goods or commodities), personal business ventures, real estate, among so many avenues.

Since this book is all about creating financial capacity for investments, I will not delve into the 'how' for each of these investment avenues. However, I will highlight the need for you to make deliberate efforts to study and understand the subjects of finance and investments. It is also important to seek wisdom and advice from the experts in these areas, and one way is by reading books on these subjects. You may also wish to talk to family, friends, and colleagues who may already be active in the various investment domains. It is good to learn from people who know what they are doing.

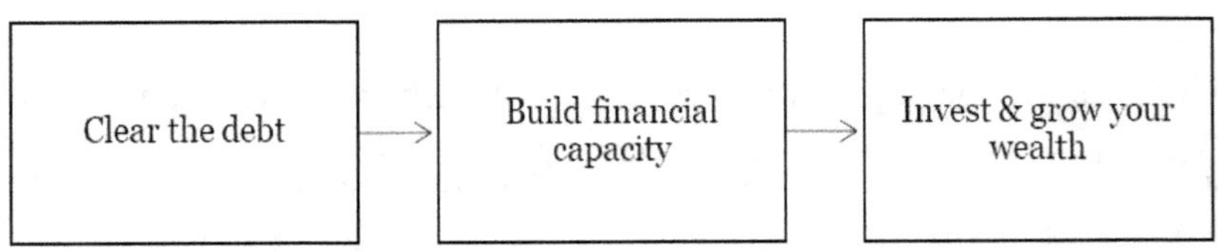

After regaining your freedom from debt, make sure you stay free. Most importantly, never assume financial freedom sets you on another path for debt-entanglement.

#don'tleaveyourmoneybehind

Making Money

"Demystify the art of making money and learn how to keep some"

8

Chapter 8: Making & Keeping Money

Many readers will agree that saving money is not the easiest thing, and for most people it does not simply come as second nature due to their unique upbringing. Most homes do not sit around the table or the fireplace discussing money, nor pondering on what keeping money can do to our lives and posterity.

For kids, the only most likely 'lesson-on-the-job' obtained whilst growing-up relate to spending. Upon reaching the age of five, our parents would usually send us to the community mini shops to grab a packet of sugar or a loaf of bread. That trend was helpful for us to appreciate currency and the power of money. We quickly became professionals in skillfully dividing the notes and the coins. However, the nebulous attributes of money remained veiled from our eyes. We did not fully comprehend that these notes are a mere representation of the real value, and if handled skillfully we could both preserve the hidden value and do massive exploits with money.

The 'get and spend' mentality was building up in our psyche without really educating us how money can be made beyond our parents or without a job. Remember we also could connect the dots. We saw dad and mom leaving the house every morning claiming that they were going to work – and we would later in the evening see them coming back home exhausted and carrying the paper bag containing essential groceries. We correctly understood that their jobs earned them money, and the money was critical for our shelter, food, dressing, some fun and general survival.

With that background, we got older, and like dad and mom we also got into a job with the mentality to live well, change the wardrobe, pump- up the kitchen, drive well, smell well, talk well, and do everything 'money-well'.

A small percentage gets into this season of life already equipped with the necessary knowledge and wisdom to manage their monetary affairs with dexterity and generational mindset.

And then our lives quickly slide through the slopes until we are 10 to 40 years in a job when we realize, yeeks! We did not keep the money! Where did it all go?!

For someone who started a job receiving US$5,000 per month and getting only 5% annual increments - if they had the discipline of saving 20% every month for the last 10 years (with no investments at all), they would be having at least US$150,000 in their bank account today. And if we assume that they started with a salary of US$10,000 on the same terms, they would be having around US$ 300,000. A simple doubling, right?

If the one getting US$10,000 monthly salary ever dared to place the funds in a risky investment earning them a modest fixed 10% per year, they would have above US$ 0.5 million!

For the love of talking in numbers, see the simplified calculation model below:

Years	Incremental Monthly Salary (US$)	No. of Months	Annual Salary (US$)	Annual Savings @20% (US$)	Cumulative Fixed Interest@ 10% (US$)
1	10,000	12	120,000	24,000	26,400
2	10,500	12	126,000	25,200	56,760
3	11,025	12	132,300	26,460	91,542
4	11,576	12	138,915	27,783	131,258
5	12,155	12	145,861	29,172	176,473
6	12,763	12	153,154	30,631	227,814
7	13,401	12	160,811	32,162	285,974
8	14,071	12	168,852	33,770	351,718
9	14,775	12	177,295	35,459	425,895
10	15,513	12	186,159	37,232	509,440
		Totals	**1,509,347**	**301,869**	**509,440**

For the sake of the theme of this book, I have tried to use simple analogies and have also avoided complex calculations. If you sit with a seasoned financial advisor, they will take you through the accounting and regulatory requirements in the applicable jurisdiction, and such matters would include varying types of investment assets, applicable taxes, and bank charges or commission. Most banks have experienced investment and wealth management teams. However, even after applying the applicable taxes and bank costs to your periodic interest, you will keep some reasonable amounts compared to someone who gobbled up all their income.

For me, being an African child, born and raised in Malawi, I grew up in the beautiful African extended family system where I had the privilege of being raised and financially supported by my uncles and aunties (together with my cousins, nephews, and a string of other wonderful people we just knew were family). In Africa everyone can be family, and the culture demands that your money finds its way to support everyone as long as you earn something. I am also aware that in some cultures the story is not vastly different. Hence, without ignoring the fact that our money has a lot of pockets to fill, we still need to be wiser on how we help others and in what we do with the rest of the cash.

A workable solution may be prioritizing giving, offerings, family support, home running, paying-off debt (if still entangled), and seriously consider setting aside funds purely for savings. Investments will be birthed from the savings, although some people recommend separating savings and investment cash at the onset. To be honest, there is no 'one' solid formula as we all have unique circumstances;

just make sure whatever your approach, save some money. The higher the percentage the better.

Countless times my bank account has asked me where all my salaries went. Till date I have no clue. All I can say is that I know the pain of being broke.

The Seasons of Life (Single or Married)

For those who are not yet married, it is important to get wiser quickly in order to take advantage of the default 'singleness of mind'. This is the time you can do all you want with your money, except for some unavoidable family support requirements in case you help your parents and support siblings or other relations. Nevertheless, this is the best time to stash away a great percentage from your salary. In fact, this is also the best time to attempt audacious business goals as you still have time to *'fail & recover'* without destroying all prospects and your mental health.

Do not be pulled away by peer-pressure and clueless friends. Think big and dare the unimaginable. This mindset is possible when you stay away from the noise and fashionable clutter; do not try to prove a point through looks and cars - don't be forced into early financial loans. Trust God and trust the process.

I am writing from experience.

When you get married, you bring into your life another soul and mind which invisibly become intertwined with yours. Your decisions start to have a different basis and you normally have an in-house committee for decision making.

I have found power in both settings. When you are alone it is easier to be 'foolishly' audacious and attempt the unimaginable. This behavior can both ruin and boost your prospects for massive gains.

When you get married, most of the 'foolish' audacity is trimmed before it even sees the light. This is especially common with men. I have never understood how our brains are coined but we are the usual suspects for quick investment decisions which burn our hands repeatedly – and we never learn. The wives act like the fact checkers or thermostats – and sometimes extremely so, *that it makes life too hard for men to just breathe and act on opportunities with spontaneity.*

I am not sure whether this trimming of potential is good. I do not know. But what I know is that women are blessed with deep intuition and greater risk management skills than men. On the other hand, men are born a little careless and ruthless with risk taking. Men are naturally bold towards risky opportunities – and one breakthrough is all we need to become successful. An optimal combination of our varying traits is the formula for success. Don't be extreme on either side. Be rational, collaborate, appreciate, understand, empathize, love, respect, and live the dream.

In extreme circumstances, one side must win based on a higher spiritual inspiration that the other party could not perceive. The outcome will still see both spouses richer and better.

Visibly, for married folks, financial decisions may not be the easiest unless you are in one of those 'military' marriages where it's my way or the highway!

If you are in a balanced relationship, you will agree that any decision requiring cash flow, demands deep preparations and tact before you explain to your husband or wife. It's a normal process called 'unity of spirit', as doing anything through the backdoor feels like you are stealing; and making forceful and irrational decisions merely creates a prison within your own home *(I know a few people can relate. I can't be the only culprit).* Investment decisions, family support, external business partnerships, etc. should be tabled and explained at home for the sake of the long-haul. No one has your back like your spouse. That is why you trust that person to the extent of allowing them to sleep beside you daily; and you know they sometimes wake up in the night (whilst you are snoring), looking at you with fiery eyes. This is just for your information.

Developing Your Own Primary Financial Statements

Accounting is easy; not just because I am a Certified Chartered Accountant, but because every complex subject has a simpler way of explaining it to a layman. Albert Einstein once said, *"If you can't explain it simply, you don't understand it well enough."*

In the world of accounting and financial reporting, the primary financial statements are the profit & loss statement (or income & expenditure), statement of financial position (or balance sheet), cash flow statement (or cash utilization), and the statement of equity (or shareholders' wealth).

For the purposes of our subject, I will show how we all can complete a simple statement of financial position and profit & loss statement. I encourage you to go through this exercise and see where you stand on your path to achieving financial freedom.

The statement of financial position shows how much money, tangible assets, intangible assets, and liabilities you have. It presents your financial health or what we can also call your 'wealth-capacity'. If you walk through your own statement of financial position, you will not be confused whether you are financially sorted or not. The below table presents the components of a standard financial position statement:

Component	Professional description	Our simplified personal description
Tangible Current Assets	Readily available items that are either cash, or can easily be converted to cash within a period of one year, e.g., stocks, short-term bank deposits, convertible money market investment papers.	Bank or household cash, and one-year-long redeemable investments, e.g., fixed deposits, repurchase agreements, etc.
Tangible Fixed Assets	Useable assets not available for sale or disposal beyond a one-year period, e.g. properties, motor vehicles, heavy equipment, etc.	Land, houses, commercial properties, motor vehicles, valuable electronics, etc.
Intangible Assets*	An identifiable non-monetary asset without physical substance, e.g., trademarks, patents, licenses, royalty, franchisee agreements, import quotas, marketing rights, customer and supplier relationships, etc.	Owned business trademarks, patents, royalties, licenses, import rights, societal goodwill, etc.

Current Liabilities	Borrowed funds, pending supplier payments, staff salaries, other contingent (or expected) cash obligations to be paid back within one-year.	Any loans, other legally binding cash obligations (e.g., credit purchases, lease-to-own obligations, litigation charges), or cash guarantees, to be settled within one-year.
Long Term Liabilities**	Similar liabilities like the short-term ones but with payment obligations beyond one-year period. This includes significant bank loans used to purchase both current and fixed assets.	Bank or family loans, lease-to-own obligations, or litigation charges falling due in a period over one-year from today. This includes mortgages and vehicle financing obligations.
Equity or Shareholders' Capital**	The business capital invested by the business owners.	Personal money used to invest in the owned current and fixed assets.

**Although beneficial and a possible conduit to make money, it is usually difficult to attribute actual monetary value to intangible assets, hence not commendable to use this component in personal financial position assessment.*

***Assets are usually financed by either your own money, say a salary, or bank loans. Since the salary is your money, it is considered as 'equity', whilst the loan must be paid back someday, and is a liability.*

A perfect statement of financial position reconciles with this formula:

Total Assets = Equity + Liabilities

Although you may have understood the difference between assets and liabilities from other personal finance literature, in corporate accounting, liabilities also help to finance the acquisition of assets, hence they are part of the total assets' formula illustrated above.

Before jumping into the excitement of making and keeping money, it is imperative to understand and appreciate how your own financial position looks like. I would advise you to take some time to conduct this exciting activity of building your own statement of financial position. The results will either make you laugh, shock you, or just lead you to a moment of self-reflection. I always consider this activity a powerful tool to jump-start effective financial planning.

See the below simplified personal statement of financial position:

Components	**US$**
Current Assets:	
Cash In Bank	30,000
Cash In Hand (In the House)	500
Repurchase Agreement (Repo)	5,500
Total Current Assets	**36,000**
Fixed Assets:	
Family Home (Street 2, Northside) *(Depreciated Value)*	102,500
Farmland (Street 4, Southside)	55,000
Land Rover 3 2010 Model *(Depreciated Value)*	5,000
Toyota Yaris 2020 Model	18,000
Three Samsung TV Sets	1,200
Kitchen & Home Equipment	3,500
Total Fixed Assets	**185,200**
Total Assets	**221,200**

Current Liabilities	
Employee (House-help) Gratuity	1,200
Bank Overdraft Balance	10,500
Family Loan Balance	16,300
Credit Card No. 1 Balance	10,000
Total Current Liabilities	**38,000**
Long Term Liabilities	
Mortgage Balance	36,500
Personal Bank Loan Balance	25,000
Automotive Loan Balance	16,000
Credit Card No. 2 Balance	12,500
Total Long-Term Liabilities	**90,000**
Total Liabilities	**128,000**
Personal Investment in Assets (a.k.a. Equity)	**93,200**
Total Investment & Liabilities	**221,200**

By simply completing this exercise, for example, you will see that although you 'own' US$221,200 worth of assets, 58% of the cash used to finance those assets (US$128,000) is owed to the bank and other family connections. Ultimately you are obligated to settle the underlying loans within a period of a year or more. Simply put, the equivalent sum of money must be paid back to the owners someday.

The quest for undertaking this exercise is to provide you the reality of where you stand regarding financial emancipation. Once you see the heaviness of your liabilities, you stand in a better position to plan the repayment plans whilst building the 'equity' side to ensure you quickly become the full owner of your assets without losing a good night's sleep.

The plan is to dwindle liabilities as much as possible and increase your cash, investments, and other assets. Liquid assets such as cash are crucial for short-term financial demands plus spotting of investment opportunities, whilst the investments are crucial for multiplying your wealth reserves. The more you effectively invest in money- making assets, the more money you can earn and keep. The combined understanding of the chapters in this book will ensure the efficacy of the money formula proposed throughout the pages.

The second financial statement is the profit and loss statement, but we will adopt its similar term 'income and expenditure statement' to properly align with our personal financial planning agenda.

The income and expenditure statement shows us how much money we make versus the periodic expenditures supported by such income. By the end of the day, the statement shows us the remaining income, which is called profit in business circles, but we will use the equivalent phrase 'retained earnings' for easy understanding and better applicability.

This statement can be completed monthly against your family budgets or indeed on an annual basis to match the retained earnings with the cash available in your bank account or in your house. Between the lines of earned income and the expenditure, there are other payments which were cushioned by credit cards, overdrafts, and personal loans. This additional financing is reflected within the above statement of financial position.

Let us review the sample income and expenditure statement below:

Components	**US$**
Income:	
Annual Salary	131,507
Annual Bonus	13,151
Interest Earned from Investments	9,500
Dividends From Partnership	55,000
Total Annual Income	**209,158**
Expenditure	
Annual House Rent	39,452
Children's School Fees	27,123
Personal Educational Costs	25,000
Motor Vehicle Maintenance	3,500
General Home Maintenance Expenses	1,500
Kitchen Equipment	3,500
Utilities	2,466
Groceries	11,507
Holidays	10,500
Other Family Support	12,500
Charity	16,000
Professional Memberships	1,000
Health Club Subscriptions	9,315
Ancillary Medical Expenses	6,500
Miscellaneous	8,795
Total Annual Expenditure	**178,658**
Retained Earnings (Remaining Cash Balance) *	**30,500**

NOTE: The retained earnings amount matches the total cash balances in your bank account and cash in hand as presented on the statement of financial position. However, please note that for corporations, the retained earnings amount does not necessarily match the amount in their bank accounts as company profit is driven by so many varying components beyond remaining cash; hence, for companies, they are also required to show their cashflow statement which presents the true picture of their available cash as of the date of reporting. We will not go to this complex path for the sake of our 'sanity and joy'.

The journey of making and saving money is like a marathon. If your financial accounts are in the negative today, you do not need to stress yourself over rushed decisions and getting worried on bygones.

Jackie Joyner-Kersee, a former American Athlete once said, "It's better to look ahead and prepare, than to look back and regret".

If you are deeply in debt or feel you are far behind in your quest to build an enviable cash and investments portfolio, do not despair. Do not fall into the trap of comparing yourself with your peers who seem to have their act together. It is okay to learn from people but always remember that we are all on our unique life journeys – and our circumstances are obviously different.

Understand:

- Some people have huge families to support, whilst others only have themselves to entertain.

- Some people inherited fortunes from their parents, whilst others never even knew the definition of inheritance.

- Some families have all well-to-do and highly educated siblings, whilst for some, they are the only progressive sibling out of a battalion.

- Some people obtained financial literacy from the age of five, whilst others only got to understand the power of money well after their fortieth birthday.

- Some people endure tough life-threatening experiences such as health problems that demand all their financial resources, whilst others have never been on this path.

- Some people have ailing and elderly parents to take care of, whilst others either already lost their parents; or their parents are well-off.

- Some have made major investment mistakes that saw them lose all their life savings, whilst others only kept a low profile with a regular savings account.

- Some invested in growth start-ups or speculative investments which made them 'overnight' millionaires, whilst some grinded their way through traditional investments that took 10 years to yield real profit. Unfortunately, some invested in 'speculative' investments and lost everything. It is called life lessons.

Only the Creator understands why each one of us has to go through a unique path. Probably it is based on the kind of calling and purpose on your life. We are called to achieve varying purposes of life and such calling demands unique training. The more you compare yourself to others the more you veer away from your chosen path. Stay on the grind. Keep your eyes forward. *Never let your hands off the plough.*

If we focus on the main game, something must give. Some people have called this 'the law of averages', entailing that the more you do something (or work hard on multiple fronts), somehow, one or many of your efforts must yield success.

In other words, the law of averages is the commonly held belief that a particular outcome or event will, over certain periods of time, occur at a frequency that is similar to its probability. Others tout the law of large numbers, which is a real theorem that states that the average of the results obtained from many trials should be close to the expected value and will tend to become closer as more trials are performed.

The law of large numbers is important because it "guarantees" stable long-term results for the averages of random events. It does not guarantee what will happen with a small number of events. *(Lumen – Boundless Statistics, The Law of Averages)*

If we genuinely want to make and save money, it's not always about massive and earth-shaking investments. The small daily steps yield exponential results. Below are some of the worthwhile lessons if you genuinely want to cause a shift in your finances:

- Do not spend or support people based on emotions. Make the calculations and see if your family can help without straining your own survival and savings. Anything can be negotiated, controlled, or explained.

- Learn delayed gratification; something like a car or TV set, or new sofa set, is not urgent. If you do not have cash, check if it makes financial sense to use debt for such purchases. Even if you have cash, wait and count the opportunity cost. It does not mean that debt is always bad – but it comes at a cost and the benefits thereof must outweigh such cost.

- The mantra remains 'don't spend what you do not have'. **All good debt is bad debt until you can attach true value to your actions**. This is a brutal truth that people can bet their whole life just to argue and prove to you why debt is good. But I hope you capture the oxymoron.

- If you take debt, always make sure the money goes into a tangible asset that can be disposed at an equal or greater value – or otherwise be able to reconcile the benefits with the related opportunity loss you could have incurred if you failed to utilize a loan in your present circumstances.

- Don't do 'I Owe Yous' in the family. For example, just because the wife bought a US$700 suit for an interview it does not mean the husband deserves a US$900 suit for the office. Match expenditures with the season and functionality; check if it is the right time to make that huge purchase – and assess if the underlying intention is aligning with the immediate or near-term purpose?

- Whatever you buy, from cars, furniture to groceries, always have the patience to check if you can get the same or similar thing from somewhere cheaper.

- Always look at functionality before making purchases. Will the item meet the intended objectives? For example, you may restrain yourself from purchasing a BMW because a cheaper car brand would still meet your comfort needs, safety, and moderate status. However, if the functionality you are chasing is comfort, safety, and a dose of luxury, then definitely your concern moves towards full-option and expensive vehicles. By expensive I mean both the purchase price and maintenance costs.

I have added the definition of 'expensive' to ensure I adequately encapsulate my sentiments. I have lived in jurisdictions where, depending on the year-of-make, second-hand Mercedes-Benz, BMW, Porsche, Maserati and Land

Rover are cheaper than used Toyota Land Cruiser or Nissan Patrol Platinum. However, the post-purchase maintenance costs can easily take a strange turn and end up proving otherwise. These 'machines' can be expensive to maintain.

- It is always better to make key purchases in line with the financial and economic season of your life. If your bank account or investments are not yet self-sustaining, opt to have restraint in acquiring liabilities disguised as assets. Simple mistakes can erode your bank account. Learn not to make temporary decisions that have permanent adverse effects on your financial freedom.

The following are some of the random pieces of advice collected from Expats who participated in a targeted survey which was conducted as part of this book project. The task was for them to share their advice to a fresh Expat *(more like giving advice to their younger selves)*. The similarities indicate resonating sentiments among the survey participants. I guess repetition never hurts!

1. Avoid loans.

2. (Name withheld) is known as the city of dreams. If you're ready to take risks and work hard, you can earn good money and have a luxurious life. Same way, in the initial stage if you did not plan/control and focus on your spending, you will get trapped with loans/credit cards.

3. Save money.

4. Enjoy a lot but still save more.

5. Save save save!!!!

6. Embrace whichever culture you are in.

7. Always be calculative when spending. One should have a clear track of monthly expenses. Always follow a strategy of first saving a specific portion of monthly salary and then meet the required expenses, rather than saving after spending. Never be fully dependent on end of service benefits alone.

8. Live within your means and spend wisely.

9. Live very modestly and spend less.

10. It is all in your luck and destiny. Just pray hard for that to be in your favor.

11. Have an investment plan and make a commitment to save a portion of your salary.

12. Start saving as soon as possible from the little you are getting.

13. Buy residential land and build a house back home.

14. After saving, start buying commercial land and slowly start building even with overseas loans. The earlier the better.

15. Have multiple savings divided into fees, investment, and retirement.

16. The joy ride can end tomorrow. Save.

17. Start saving early and avoid unnecessary expenditure.

18. Find ways to save even a little at a time.

19. Live within your means!

20. Maintain your home country's low lifestyle to save enough money and then adjust it gradually with time.

21. Move overseas with minimum 3 to 5 years of experience and do not join as fresher.

22. Exchange rate looks fancy on the calculator. Consider all living expenses before accepting any job offer.

23. Two things on choosing an overseas role: please do your research, no assumptions whatsoever, then do your math.

24. Live within your means. Set target savings and budget wisely. Spend on the essentials and do not forget to treat yourself sometimes.

25. Bless others with the blessings you receive whether big or small.

26. Do not get stressed with money whenever you lose it for any reason (e.g., an investment that fails or helping others). You can earn it again.

27. Prioritize what matters in life and do not make money the main deciding factor.

28. Have a targeted timeframe and work diligently towards it, start immediately.

29. Make an investment.

30. Make sure you are not carried away with the leisure of

overseas.

31. Any amount is worth saving and save every day by cutting down on leisure.

32. Make your financial goal and life milestones (e.g., marriage, owning a house, investments, etc.) and then do your expenses. However, enjoy your life to the utmost.

33. Focus on your targets and spend wisely.

34. Research well enough before finalizing the pay with employer.

35. Do not get a bank loan, do not get a credit card.

36. Financial stability is not determined by how much you take home monthly. It's rather determined by how much you save, even from the smallest salary or wage that you receive. Financial discipline needs to be always adhered to in order to succeed.

37. Rely on yourself, friends will not be there for you, plan well before traveling.

38. Be determined and live within your ability.

39. Do not borrow money from the bank.

40. Do not spend what you have not earned.

41. The motivation to go abroad should not be primarily money. In terms of disposable income, you may probably be better off as a local staff than an expatriate, but it really depends on your nature of the job.

42. Do not get over excited, take your time and understand how the markets work and the implications of getting a credit facility and do proper research into what you want to invest your money in to ensure you are in line with your goals.

43. Know what you need and why you are traveling.

44. Enjoy it as well as save.

45. Set reasonable expectations and do your research before joining an overseas employer. Visit if possible.

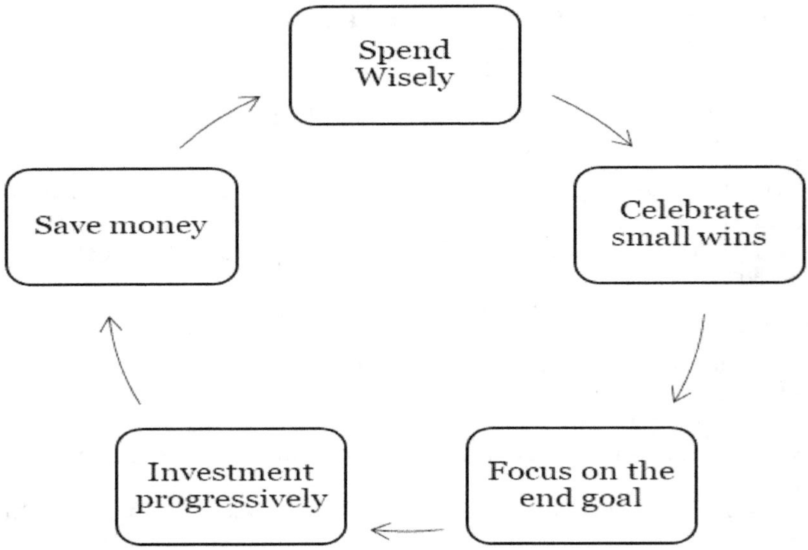

Investment Options

The world is not short of investment opportunities, and I've come to appreciate that each one of us has our own unique preferred investment vehicles. That said, this book will not be complete if I don't delve into the common investment options that can preserve and grow your wealth.

By definition:

- *"Wealth is an accumulation of valuable economic resources that can be measured in terms of either real goods or money value.*

- *Net worth is the most common measure of wealth, determined by taking the total market value of all physical and intangible assets owned, then subtracting all debts.*
- *The concept of wealth is usually applied only to scarce economic goods; goods that are abundant and free for everyone provide no basis for relative comparisons across individuals.*
- *Unlike income, which is a flow variable, wealth measures the amount of valuable economic goods that have been accumulated at a given point in time.*
- *The relative differences in wealth between people are what we usually refer to in order to define who is wealthy or not."*

  -Investopedia

Below are some of the common investment options you may want to place your money:

Real Estate

Various finance and investment literature refer to Real Estate as land together with the permanent structures built on such land (i.e. property). Property comes in all forms, shapes, sizes, and utilizations. The common terminology is either 'residential' or 'commercial' property; the former being for personal or family accommodation whilst the latter is used for business lease. You can build or buy residential homes for your family usage but also for leasing to residential tenants. But you can also opt to develop warehouses, shops, malls, plazas, towers, et al, for business leasing.

Others opt to simply invest in massive agricultural land for current or later productive use or leasing. Land can also be maintained for capital appreciation purposes.

Now, this is how people make money from real estate. Property leasing provides you periodic income through the monthly or annual rentals, whilst the land and buildings preserve value which allows you to double or even triple the purchase value through an 'opportunistic' sale. It is true that property prices can tumble due to some economic recession or a periodic industry bubble, but the beauty of owning property is that the assets are tangible and always hold the hope that the market will at some point bounce back. The only challenge occurs if you are financing your acquisitions through bank debt, and you need to swim- through massive loan repayments during a bubble. Nevertheless, this reality should not stifle your desire to own property.

My duty in this book is to open your eyes to the possibilities that money can create, and not necessarily to delve into the subject of comparative investment channels. This book will not tell you the crux of real estate such as how to get the best deals, property valuation, or associated costs (i.e., insurance, tax, city rates, maintenance, etc.). There are numerous books on these subjects. My encouragement will be for you to take time and invest in good investment and finance management books. Applied knowledge can work miracles in a span of 5 to 10 years. Nevertheless, following is the summary of the common ways to invest in real estate: rental properties (discussed above), Real Estate Investment Trusts (REITs), real estate limited partnerships, real estate investment groups, real estate mutual funds, and flipping houses.

REITs are publicly traded trusts that own and manage rental properties. They can own anything: medical office space, malls, industrial real estate, and office or apartment buildings, among so many investment avenues.

Real Estate Investment Groups maintain the practice of purchasing and managing properties and then selling off parts of the property to investors. These are groups made up of friends or partners who develop the property together with the objective of spinning it off to willing buyers. However, the operating group retains a portion of the rent and manages the property. The group finds new tenants and takes care of all maintenance.

House flipping involves buying, repairing, and selling - or buying, holding, and selling. Although considered a risky affair, house flipping can also be more profitable. The fundamental approach is to ensure you get a good bargain on the purchase price and restrict the repair and renovation costs to as low amounts as possible. You only make good money if your resale price is reasonably higher than the combined costs for buying, repairing, and renovating.

Capital Markets

Capital markets are platforms through which both individuals and companies trade different types of financial instruments. These platforms include the stock market, currency and foreign exchange markets, and bond markets, apart from other evolving innovative means.

People and entities seeking funding go to the above platforms to get capital for their businesses, be it in equity (shareholding) or debt. The investors usually have surplus cash which they decide to either purchase equity of preferred companies, or give it to the government or private entities in form of bonds, or indeed trade on the foreign exchange market buy (simply) buying foreign currencies that are deemed to be performing well or even 'hoped to perform well against other global currencies', with the hope of selling them-off against some weakening currency which will allow the 'trader' to make more money out of such trades.

Unlike the stock market, where you can buy or sell a single stock, the currency market is by default designed to ensure trading is done in pairs; you should buy one currency and sell another currency in the forex market. A high-level review of currency trading will indicate that most of the trade volumes are confined to only 18 currency pairs, contrasted to the numerous stocks that are available in the global equity markets. According to Investopedia, *"although there are other traded pairs outside of the 18, the eight currencies most often traded are the U.S. dollar (USD), Canadian dollar (CAD), euro (EUR), British pound (GBP), Swiss franc (CHF), New Zealand dollar (NZD), Australian dollar (AUD) and the Japanese yen (JPY)".*

In early 2022, Statista, a reliable online portal providing data on the global digital economy, industrial sectors, consumer markets, public opinion, media and macroeconomic trends, reported that the New York Stock Exchange was the largest in the world boasting of market capitalization of listed companies over 27 trillion United States Dollars. The other leading stock exchanges within the Top 10 were NASDAQ (USA), Shanghai Stock Exchange (China), Euronext (Europe), Japan Exchange Group (Japan), Shenzhen Stock Exchange (China), Hong Kong Exchanges (Hong Kong), LSE Group (UK), National Stock Exchange of India (India), and TMX Group (Canada) - *statista.com*.

A focused approach to study these markets and access platforms that would allow you to buy company stocks would be a great way to start. The good news is that many banks have in-house investment teams that can advise you the best way to go about international stock trading, where the banks usually offer to manage your investment, or they may simply provide you access to your own trading platform (application) where you can manage your own investment portfolio. These applications may also allow you to trade in commodities, forex, and cryptocurrencies, apart from the common company stocks. If you don't understand investments, it is commendable to trust the bank's investment managers or other external fund management companies to help with your portfolio management. However, due to some strange commissions, management fees, and transactional fees, experienced investors opt to manage their own portfolios over time. Apart from the big international stock exchanges, most progressive economies also boast of their own national stock exchanges where some of the local and regional prestigious firms are listed, and you can opt to buy shares in these companies rather than chasing Facebook and Google Shares on the NYSE. Most of the stock exchange websites provide the lists and contacts of accredited 'stockbrokers'. A stockbroker is a licensed professional with the authority to buy and sell stocks for other investors. Stockbrokers are regulated by the local financial markets regulators and are typically employed by a brokerage or a broker-dealer. Stockbrokers work on commission and usually receive a percentage of the trade's value as their fee.

A good Stockbroker will also provide you with investment advice and conduct market research to understand the trajectory of the stocks and markets. In a big way, I have realized that some of the best investment advice is obtained, not from the professional traders, but rather from your colleague sitting across the cubicle, or your next-door neighbor. My advice to you would be to talk to the active investors within your circles before you plunge yourself into the 'profit oriented' maze of financial markets.

Money Markets

These markets deal in assets that are bought and sold on short term basis, with maturities ranging from a day to a year, and are also easily convertible into cash. The common money market instrument is a bank deposit – followed by term certificates of deposit; interbank loans (loans between banks); money market mutual funds; commercial paper; treasury bills; and securities lending and repurchase agreements (repos).

Another common and 'safest' (low risk) investment are the treasury bills issued by the government, also commonly having maturities of less than a year. Most entities and individuals utilize treasury bills as a profitable means for saving surplus funds.

Randall Dodd, a former advisor in the IMF's Monetary and Capital Markets Department, described Repos as large, but more complicated segment of money markets. "Repos offer competitive interest rates for borrowing and lending on a short-term basis—usually no more than two weeks and often overnight. A borrower sells a security it owns for cash and agrees to buy it back from the purchaser (who is in effect a lender) at a specified date and at a price that reflects the interest charge for borrowing over the period. The security at the heart of the transaction serves as collateral for the lender."

To benefit from the money markets, it is imperative to seek advice from, again, friends, colleagues, and neighbors who are already busy making money from the various securities offered in this segment. If the only instrument you've been making interest from is your bank account, you've not really understood the time value for money. Even if you run fixed deposit accounts, the comparative interest rates would not match the plethora of the other money market instruments.

Beyond inquiring from personal contacts, at least showing some interest and making the moves, your bankers are also a crucial source of information, apart from the numerous independent fund managers.

CHAPTER 8

Private Business

This one is my favorite. I love this space because you can invest your money in avenues that align with your own passions, especially involving building something from the ground. For me, personally, I just love to get my hands dirty and feel the sense of pride that I am doing something worthwhile.

Don't get me wrong, if you are a good investor, and you also have the money and means to go big on stock markets you will mint more cash than the average business owner on the street; but it is also good to create some personal space where you utilize all your senses to build something beautiful. It could be something as simple as a coffee shop, or an eatery, a library, or an events garden – whatever would give you a good sense of satisfaction. Maybe it's just me, after all!

Private businesses can either be a sole proprietorship which is run solely by you or your family; or it can be a partnership where you pool resources and share equity between two, or among more partners. You can also create a bigger limited liability company where the equity can be held by several partners, or indeed owned solely by one person but where the company bears its own legal personality, and its affairs are managed by a fully-fledged management team who report to the board of directors. Each type of business is governed by a different set of rules in accordance with the company registry and commercial laws in your jurisdiction. You may need to find a good lawyer to offer you advice on the type of businesses you can create plus the pros and cons for each of the available options.

Big ideas are not monopolized. With great partnerships, knowledge, understanding, and the right environment, I believe anyone can create a thriving enterprise in any major business sector in your country. Although it sounds like a cliché, it is true that money will always follow big ideas. There are numerous testimonies of people in the telecoms, energy, mining, consumer goods, health care, real estate, entertainment, among many sectors, who have ventured into these areas by embracing diversity in partnerships, understanding the global financing network, soliciting, or lobbying government support, and moving to the right jurisdictions.

Talking to various business owners and investors, I've learnt that the best and most enjoyable experiences are gained when you align business with your passions. There are some things we do just because we can get quick money, but there are also things we can do because we simply love to do them. My advice will be to have both types of businesses within your portfolio. You at least need to have a business that can be a cash cow, meaning the one that gives you more liquidity (cash) that you can use to build and develop other passions. In the simplest sense, one money-making business that secures your bread and butter. Based on how much liquidity is available to you, you can now have more space to get creative and innovative with the hope of building a mini-unicorn that would possibly show signs of success in the next 5 to 10 years.

Recently I've been fascinated by the profitability of street food stands; you will be shocked how much money the food peddlers make. Some of them only sell a cup of tea or coffee plus one hot-selling snack (it could be chicken pie or samosa). Without demeaning the challenges faced by some the food vendors, and the stark realities of poverty in some circles, if an average vendor sales a combo of tea and snacks at 50 cents to 500 customers, he will make US$250 per day – which translates to US$7,500 per month (30 days) – and US$90,000 per year. These numbers can be tweaked to accommodate less business days, city council fees, or taxes if applicable. Then you can also estimate the profit and loss calculations by applying, say, 40% of running costs. If we remove 20% tax, 5% city council fees, and 60% materials and operating costs, our sample vendor will take home an annual profit of

US$13,500.

These small businesses, however, work on volumes. If you run food stalls in China, India, Nigeria, Egypt, Philippines, and Bangladesh, you have a higher probability of pulling in the crowds compared to low population countries like Nauru, Tuvalu, Palau, and San Marino. However, if you are competitive enough you can still make money, anywhere. People will always need food and other necessities in life. For every business idea, you will need to patiently go through adequate research, due diligence, and counsel. Make sure you obtain as much counsel as possible and ultimately make your own decision. You must learn to follow your own instincts and hold yourself accountable for your decisions. It's not honorable to mess up and forever keep on pointing fingers at someone you believe gave you wrong advice. Of course, some people can deliberately sabotage a good opportunity, but in the business world you need to learn to make bold decisions.

Among numerous brilliant publications, some of the most touted relevant books on the subjects of finance and investments include: Millionaire Expat and Millionaire Teacher by Andrew Hallam; You Can Be A Stock Market Genius By Joel Greenblatt; The Intelligent Investor By Benjamin Graham; The Essays Of Warren Buffett; The

Warren Buffett Way By Robert Hagstrom; The Little Book Of Common Sense Investing By John C. Bogle; Rich Dad Poor Dad and The Cash Quadrant by Robert Kiyosaki; The Richest Man in Babylon by George Samuel Clason; The Total Money Makeover by Dave Ramsey; The Millionaire Next Door: The Surprising Secrets of America's Wealthy by Thomas J. Stanley; The Simple Path to Wealth by J. L. Collins; Think and Grow Rich by Napoleon Hill; Zero to One by Peter Theil; The Lean Startup by Eric Ries; The Hard Thing About Hard Things by Ben Horowitz; Trade Your Way to Financial Freedom by Van Tharp; Fooled by Randomness by Nassim Nicholas Taleb.

In my own opinion, among the so many big business ideas, in a lifetime, one must attempt to run at least one of the following businesses: a bakery, a restaurant or café, a commercial agricultural farm (animals or plants), a fashion house, food market (e.g., a mini or supermarket), or any other simple activity that puts you on the front-end of making people happy.

Whatever big dream you have, start from where you are and embrace opportunities on the way.

A Case for Entrepreneurship – A Partial Excerpt from My

2020 Publication, The Entrepreneurship Agenda

It is beyond a cliché that entrepreneurs create jobs. Yes, this is true, but in most countries private entities trail behind the public sector in job creation, and the government remains the biggest employer. Although the government can create a fertile environment for business establishments, there is limited growth potential for ministries and parastatals to absorb the ever-blossoming populations. This is where entrepreneurs come in to offer lasting employment and human development opportunities.

Entrepreneurs (mostly innovators) create novel and remodeled solutions to national challenges, and in the process usher in a dimension of learning and growth that continues to act as a snowball in the economy. Innovation leads to the creation of more innovators, and that spiral effect has the power to transform a nation. In the case of the African Continent, the best territorial beneficiaries of innovation include Rwanda, Kenya, Ghana, Morocco, and Nigeria. A strong case can be made for these economies that the presence of numerous role models in the technology, entertainment, manufacturing, and agricultural industries has led to a sporadic rise of local enterprises. And the performance of their economies is a testament to what industrial progress can do to a nation. Technological advancement is a key catalyst. The biggest testament is the American Silicon Valley which has been replicated the world over.

Of course, there is always that sentiment that not all of us can be entrepreneurs. As much as this is a sincere and candid statement, but, specifically, why not you? There is immense freedom, joy, and productivity when a person embraces a path that is less trodden with a vision to transform a community and a nation, and to become so relevant for his or her generation. Each one of us carries massive seeds of greatness that if only provided the opportunity to 'fall to the ground' our nations would be transformed beyond measure. Most great revolutions (in whatever sphere) started by the will of only one person, who then proceeded to influence a cohort with similar passions. That's how great change happens. Each one of us has a responsibility to empty our gifts and talents before we depart the surface of the earth. Why die with all the wealth hibernated inside of you and leave your nation the same way you found it?

With the modern trajectory of automation, blockchain, and the internet of things (IoT), there is no longer any denying that the world is shifting towards more efficiency and productivity, mostly driven by machines and 'code'. It doesn't matter how much we may choose to cling to the office desk, a time may soon come that most of the working class has to give up their stable careers over to the computers or some young geeks who can work wonders on tasks that were once thought as the 'holy grail' of big corporates.

One way to prepare for such a time is to start working on something that machines can only replicate but do not really satisfy all human demands. Such hidden demands are usually found in the simplest things of life as illustrated above. Beyond the simple business ideas, get on a quest to be on the side of the investors who will be pushing for the automation agenda, rather than to be on the receiving end of being replaced with the machines and code.

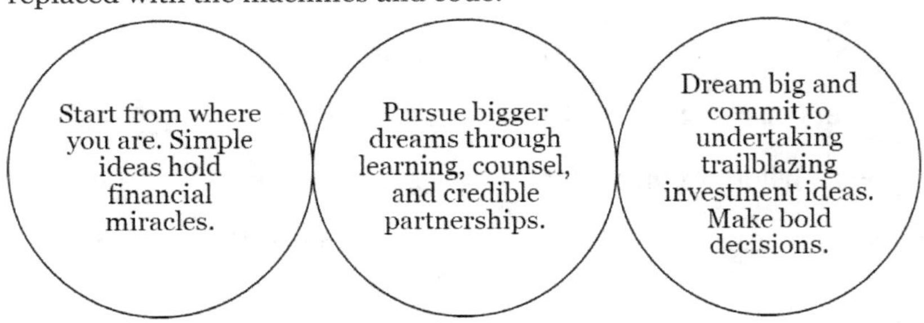

Personal Financial Statements Exercise Templates

If you are serious about understanding personal finance management, take some time to complete the personal financial statements below and see where you stand!

Simplified personal statement of finance position

Components	US$
Current Assets:	
Total Current Assets	
Fixed Assets:	
Total Fixed Assets	
Total Assets	

Current Liabilities	
Total Current Liabilities	
Long Term Liabilities	
Total Long-Term Liabilities	
Total Liabilities	
Personal Investment in Assets (aka Equity)	
Total Investment & Liabilities	

Simplified income and expenditure statement:

Components	US$
Income:	
Total Annual Income	
Expenditure	
Total Annual Expenditure	
Retained Earnings (Remaining Cash Balance)	

A Microsoft Excel-based monthly moving budget (like the below) can be utilized for budgeting and tracking your personal income and expenditures. A more detailed schedule can also be developed depending on your actual income sources and types of expenditure. The moving budgeting schedule provides you with a better picture on how the monthly income and expenditures are balancing off and adding to your overall savings and investments buckets:

Month/ Amount	Jan	Feb	Mar	Apr	May	Jun	Jul	Aug	Sept	Oct	Nov	Dec
Net Salary												
Other Income												
Total Income												
Giving												
Rental												
Groceries												
Vehicle Expenses												
School Fees												
Other Expenses												
Total Expenses												
Investments												
Savings												
Net Balance												

Note: The usual budgeting models prioritize savings and investments before making any monthly deductions to your paycheck. This approach is also endorsed by me; however, the above template is meant to provide you a deep view (or final impact) of your disbursements on the 'accumulated savings', or indeed 'accumulated deficits'. You can also choose to develop your own (more flexible) schedule based on this illustration. The investment, projects and savings buckets determine the overall investment you are making towards your future.

There is nothing like 'only one sure path for making money'. Both brilliant and silly ideas have turned simple people into multi-millionaires through grit, focus, guidance, faith, grace, and purpose. Don't lose the dream!

#don'tleaveyourmoneybehind

Family Financial Plan

"A bigger picture on family finances"

9

Chapter 9: Creating a Family Financial Plan

Despite being a unit, couples usually don't agree on everything. I know this is a strange thing to say and would even be more surprising to singles. However, this is what it is. We need to keep in mind that although a spiritual unit exists between spouses, they are still two separate living entities.

Each party to the unit still maintains their childhood dreams, passions, and desires. Both the husband and wife have unique deeper proclivities and things they wish they could have achieved somewhere (before getting married, or during the early days of the marriage). Some still hold audacious goals they wish they can achieve before they turn to that golden age. Everyone has their target.

All this uniqueness does not cease merely on the premise of this wonderful divine union called marriage. Hence, it is important for each party to the 'union' to understand these prevailing differences and to ensure we don't become the stumbling block to each other's life pursuits.

This understanding does not in any way exhort the pride in either party to establish dominance over the other, for example through more academic papers, whilst the other languishes in a meager level of educational attainment. By seeking to understand and support each other in love, any element of pride is eliminated. All acceptance is neither conformance nor compromise – it is simply love.

When it comes to matters of money and finance management, couples still face the same 'contentions' of whether money should be used for this or for the other demand; to be used now or later; to be spent or saved; to be given away or kept. Apart from what many psychology gurus have written on the subject (and I bet you've read lots of books this far), money, and not sex, could be the main cause of marital problems today. Your in-laws are not even close! Hence, it is crucial to study this issue of money with a rare passion. It is not going away anytime soon even if you choose to ignore it. If you have dominant money wrangles, I advise you to seek marital counselling from matured and financially successful older couples. You can also go to your peers or younger couples, but I would not guarantee if they have faced enough life troubles to entrust them with your 'one-life' opportunity. To mitigate the risk of fatal advice, I would insist you go to older and experienced couples.

You can also grab a few books on topics surrounding money and biological uniqueness in men and women. Something like "Men are from Mars and Women are from Venus" can do miracles. Personally, I trust the Bible on such deep and eternal subjects.

It is prudent to learn from other people's mistakes rather than waiting to make your own mistakes. You can save your marriage, and even your life, simply by humbling yourself and seeking advice from the family next door. Not literally the neighbors you don't know, but essentially from that couple that always exudes a sense of bonding

and provable financial success.

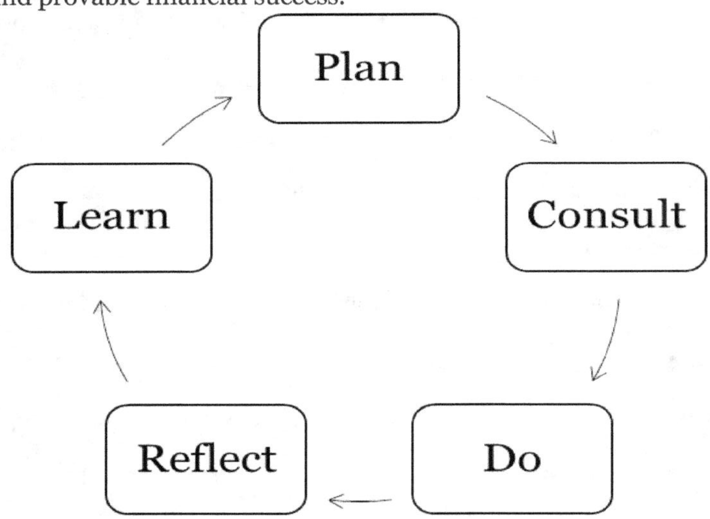

When it comes to family finance management, the solution is **not to** demarcate lines of earnings and expenditures, or to identify each one's salary or revenues as theirs alone; rather, it is critical to have a sober understanding that every income that comes into the home, through either spouse, belongs to the union; hence whether we are spending on the common needs, e.g. groceries, or on unique items for the husband, wife or kids, e.g. clothing, men's toys (sports cars), the money does not cease to belong to the family. It is still your money – hence, your costs.

The only way to win as a family in the matters of money is to develop a family financial plan.

According to smartasset™, *family financial planning is something you should be giving thought to when you're managing money for more than just yourself. Thinking long-term and planning can increase your likelihood of being able to reach your financial goals. Whether you choose to create a financial plan on your own or use an advisor, there's no better time than the present to get started.*

What A Family Financial Plan Is All About

In simple terms, a family financial plan sets out family financial responsibilities, earnings, expenditures, debt-repayments, investments, and specific savings for education, events, vacations, acquisitions, among all the wonderful things we love to have in this world.

As discussed in the preceding chapter, the first step should always be a candid assessment of the family's current financial position. This starts with listing the following items:

- The money you make monthly or annually. This includes salaries, consultancy fees or revenues from businesses;
- The average monthly or annual expenditures;
- Outstanding debt and monthly or annual target repayments;
- Fixed or varying financial commitments towards families, organizations, missions, events, or as applicable; and
- Current education commitments for the whole family.

Once these are established, it is now easy to align this reality to your desired future.

Just like the development of a simple script, you now move on to design your immediate, medium-term, and long-term financial goals. At the early attempt, there is no need for complexity. Otherwise, the process may become a burden and you stand to lose interest. Keeping it simple has been our mantra throughout this book.

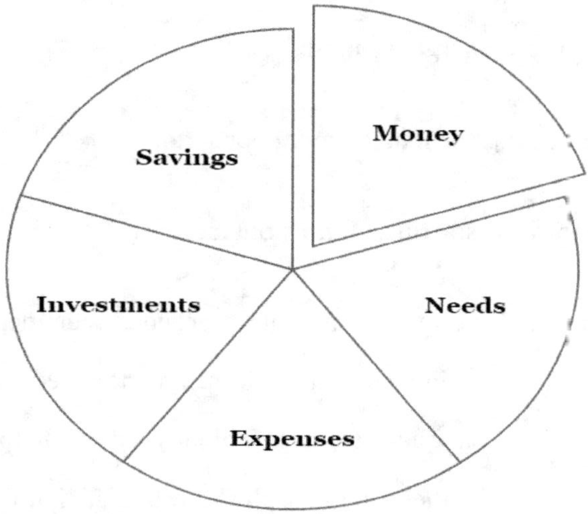

Your financial commitments may take the following shape:

- Debt repayment;
- Acquire a better and bigger family car;
- Purchase a family home;
- Build apartments for investment income;
- Save towards children's college education;
- Save towards personal advanced educational programs;

- Acquire a family farm and cottage;
- Develop an emergency fund;
- Create a long-term investment portfolio;
- Save towards starting a family business; etc.

All these desires will have specific amounts attached to them depending on your location and prevailing market prices. As indicated earlier, you may wish to involve a qualified financial advisor to help with the detailed and precise financial targets plus the overall family financial plan.

Once you have the key components figured out, you will need to come up with a better monthly and annual budgeting format using the financial reporting fundamentals from the previous chapter.

At this stage, you can list the periodic cash inflows against the immediate outflows to see how much money you will have available to fulfil all your dreams. This is not to preclude the much-touted saving strategy of 'saving first before spending'. But I am recommending an initial income-expenditure assessment to help you work backwards to arrange a reasonable expenditure-savings-investments plan. This is merely paperwork used to fire-up your financial muscles.

Since this is a family financial planning exercise, I highly recommend this process to be conducted cordially by both spouses, sometimes including your older kids depending on their comprehension. No matter the vast financial differences, it will be a futile exercise if you are not aligned as a couple. Some tough decisions such as cutting down on specific expenditures will emanate from this exercise; but if any of the spouses, for example, feels like they can't cut their gym and massage spa budget, then the whole hassle of financial planning may not bear the desired fruits.

Below is a snapshot of crystalized financial buckets which can be used for your reference. Feel free to attach some annual (amount) targets and intended periods for better perspective:

Income:

- Salary
- Commission
- Bonus
- Consulting fees
- Dividends
- Personal business earnings
- Gifts
- Returns from asset sales
- Travel allowances
- *(Insert others)*

Expenses	**Investments**	**Savings**
Home expenditure Charity Education Medical care Varying forms of insurance Debt repayments	Property Equity/share purchases Money market Family businesses Partnerships	Emergency fund Educational fund Vacation fund Cash savings
Add additional buckets below:		

If you have one salary to split across the various family interests, then you need to combine your reasonable and priority pursuits to ably assess the impact on the bottom line. This comprehensive review of your financial targets ensures that you do not overestimate the capacity of your gross pay to cover all the short-term dreams. Be clear on the calendarization of the combined plans. For instance, 'Geoffrey will commence his studies towards the Executive MBA in March 2024 with a targeted completion in February 2026 (costing us US$15,000); Mariah will commence her Master's Degree program in International Development in December 2025 with a completion target of November 2027 (costing us US$17,000)'. Such an articulate plan brings in a deeper perspective of your ambitions and a fair probability whether your immediate resources can support these 4-year educational goals.

As much as there is room for investing your early savings which may allow you to attain the financial targets quicker, the prudence principle of accounting discourages 'early recognition of profits' until realized. Accordingly, my kind advice is to work only with the tangible monthly amounts from your employment, existing projects, or other certain personal engagements. Any future earnings, bonuses or venture profits should be viewed as merely other income. This extra income is also considered as windfall, meaning not expected.

Writing down personal plans and financial goals helps you to talk in numbers. Talk is cheap when it is not tied to the corresponding numbers. Although the numbers may bring either excitement or disappointment, it is okay. It is part of the game. For example, a salary that seemed substantial and sufficient at the onset may be dwarfed by a mere writing down of your family goals. But this does not mean the overseas move completely becomes unattractive if you are not able to meet any of the short or mid-term goals. It just helps you to have a more sober reflection on your expectations. Some things can be pushed into the medium or long term as you try to sort out priorities. If you consider your spouse's education to be a priority you should be willing to postpone your own plan.

And what about the children? Especially if you have older ones who are already soldiering through high school and university. Is it clear whether they will be able to get scholarships or are you going to pay for their education? Will your employer cover the school fees until a certain age, or are you going to have to square the bills from the same salary? What does that look like? So, you also put all the specifics down, indicating that this is what you will need to undertake all these obligations, and to ultimately achieve your goals.

Once you start breaking down all these fundamentals, you will see that your financial plan will be taking shape, and you start to get a better picture of what financial freedom really looks like for your family. You now see that the monthly amount that you really need (within the targeted overseas timeline), maybe, is US$7,000 or US$15,000 to achieve the fundamentals, and this is only after considering the education component. But you need to still break it down further for all expenditures and move on to candidly look at the family investment plan. Remember the investment plan could be your main thing. Do not major in minors.

Do you have the specific savings or investment figure?

I appreciate that due to lots of 'what ifs' resting on our minds, most of us fail to establish solid goals for the fear of failure, embarrassment and frustration. But remember these targets are part of your private journal - only shared between you and your spouse, and partially with your kids where they may need to appreciate why you live the way you do, or why you do not take them to that weekly hotel event.

People would gladly apply the 'machine-gun' approach where they just shoot every bullet towards any direction, just going helter-skelter, and life happens on the go. For a few people this approach may work, whilst for the bigger cohort this approach literally hits them in the head and they later realize they've lived a long futile life, away from home. I encourage people to be very specific on what they want in terms of investment plans. You could be someone like me who gets excited about investing in everything, which is not bad – but even that 'everything' needs to be understood and be written down. So, you would say we want to establish our animal farm loaded with sheep and cattle; and this is the projected start-up capital for this farm – and you write down the amount for the farm equity, and you set a time target plus the how of the matter (the raising of funds per month, or whether you will seek external financial support). That's a good goal as discussed in Chapter 1.

Don't beat yourself by the belief that setting a specific goal might tie-you-down and you won't enjoy your life, blah blah blah. In fact, the purpose of the goal is to tie-you-down so that you stay disciplined. There is no need for you to be depressed or feel anxious that you didn't put down a lot of things that you need (as of yesterday!). Over time, one thing leads **to the other**, and then to the next thing – plus one more thing. This **'to the other'** experience happens to people who have been disciplined to the **'one thing'**. This is a truth you will notice from the great personalities of the world, from founders of unicorns to athletes, and politicians. They will initially just birth one **'breakthrough goal'** and once they've made the millions, they start pouring out the excesses into buying stock or shares in other progressive companies – and in that way they become richer and richer.

I can build a case study here for global icons like Warren Buffet, Mark Zuckerberg, Aliko Dangote, Bill Gates, Strive Masiyiwa, Ratan Tata and all the numerous billionaires and millionaires you know. If we all lead disciplined, purposeful, and visionary lives we could one day make it on the Forbes list of millionaires 'under 80', new billionaires list, most-influential people in the country, region, continent, or the globe. But it all starts with a dream, a plan, a vision, and massive discipline. *"Life doesn't just happen because you are happening"*. (Tweet that!)

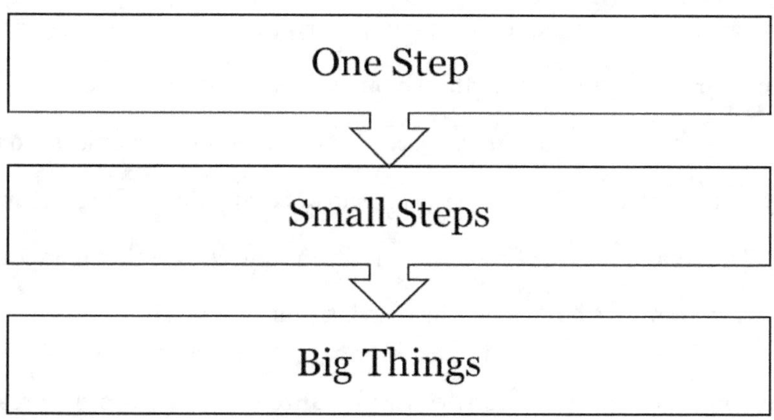

For the sake of promoting the singleness of mind, you will notice that for these famous business tycoons, one thing has led to a lot of other things. You bet they all started with one business, and many failures in between. They could not have been where they are today if they hadn't started with that one thing – that one breakthrough idea. Hence, it is crucially important to focus on one thing. That one thing for you could be your farm. Just do it well – ensure success - and later move on into other areas of your passions and interests. We will talk more about investments in a later chapter.

For the sake of this chapter, if you truly work towards an investment target within your grandeur vision, which is going to help you fulfil your purpose, whether be it a portfolio of company shares, a consulting business, a medical or legal practice, an accounting firm, or a technical motor vehicle maintenance workshop, or, better still, a beverage manufacturing venture, or anything you want to focus on – just learn to get very specific about it. Moreover, if you are coming overseas on a salary, you obviously cannot create a group of companies at the start- up point. This may be part of your grand vision, but we are talking about the start-up point. What will be the starting point for you?

As we ponder on these matters, you will realize that these are the areas that people don't usually want to talk about because this is hard work – **planning is hard work** – thinking about a plan is hard work. *That's why companies hold meetings to discuss meetings to arrange meetings in preparation for a future meeting*. People escape from the actual work! Remember, we don't rush into things that will affect our income and our future. Simple ideas and actions may destroy our entire future. Just because you are getting good money does not mean you can simply wake up one day and do a huge project No; it does not work that way. When money gets into your hands it will always find something to do because it is nebulous. It will always be led to any other open course if you do not discipline it to follow a specific course. Can you see why a plan is crucial? Your money needs to find a ready- made plan.

A family financial plan is like a financial compass that helps keep your generational sanity.

#don'tleaveyourmoneybehind

Sustained Financial Freedom

"Snippets on how to remain financially free"

10

Chapter 10: Stay Financially Free

The Art of Personal Discipline

There are many cases where former *'financial prisoners'* easily relapse into the debt trap after a moment of relief. It is not strange to see people easily getting back to their former ways despite fully knowing the pain, shame, heartache, chaos, and uneasiness of being caught in the debt trap.

I like the below extract from a classic Jim Rohn coaching session:

"What you become is far more important than what you get. The important question to ask on the job is not, what am I getting? Instead, you should ask, what am I becoming? Getting and becoming are so closely intertwined—what you become directly influences what you get. Think of it this way: Most of what you have today you have attracted by becoming the person you are now. I've also found that income rarely exceeds personal development. Sometimes income takes a lucky jump, but unless you learn to handle the responsibilities that come with it, it will usually shrink back to the amount you can handle. If someone hands you a million dollars, you'd better hurry up and become a millionaire. A very rich man once said, If you took all the money in the world and divided it equally among everybody, it

would soon be back in the same pockets it was before."

So, there it is. I believe this is true.

If all the money in the world was equally distributed among the current population (in our exact mindset, training, and understanding), all the loose spenders would quickly visit every store and give back the hard cash to the enterprising population; and soon enough we will be back to default settings.

Someone may say this is the work of 'capitalism', or we may try to blame the system for such 'one way cash traffic'. However, if the complainers choose to create their own enterprises with a view to harness the power of a capitalistic environment, soon enough other spenders will start to buy and consume their offerings, whether they are selling food, merchandize, or indeed offering a service – something like a spa, gym, play centre, consulting services, among so many business opportunities we may wish to participate in.

In my modest experience, I have seen people who once said strange things against entrepreneurs change overnight when they become business owners. They quickly metamorphosize into preachers of the gospel of entrepreneurship and how they wish everyone could become an entrepreneur. This world has strange ways.

Going back to the subject. Personal discipline entails consistency in the new value system which created possibilities for you and your family. Whether you now have made it and your bank account looks like life is happening for you, the only way to sustain the new environment and to possibly catapult yourself into the sphere of abundance is by staying on the exact course of the principles and behaviors that brought you this far.

You may be tempted to find new friends who appear to be 'happening'; but always remember our mantra, *"life doesn't happen just because you are happening"*. It is a fallacy. Keep close the friends who walked with you to freedom and ignore the ones who only join your cohort because of your financial dominance. Flirting friends will always run away the moment you lose what they came for. Stay on course.

Progressive financial freedom is like the building of muscles in a gym. You probably know of that one person (maybe it's even you) who goes to the gym once in a month and gets all busy looking at the mirrors to see if their biceps are growing and solidifying. They probably also eat lots of apples and cabbage for one week and fantasize about massive vitality and the best shape ever! A few days down the line they are already cheating on fat pizza pieces and those sumptuous chicken wings, still dreaming that soon they will have the best body. What a fantasy!

The only way you build muscle and stay on the path of vitality is by being consistent. You develop a health plan and daily routine on how you conduct your workouts, what food you eat, what motivation or inspirational talks you listen to, where you get your spiritual food, and how you sustain healthy relationships with family and friends. You may not believe it now, but your relationships also affect the way you take care of yourself. It all adds up; that's the best way I can sum it all up.

You don't stop saving your paycheck just because you believe you have saved enough; or stopping investing just because you think it looks 'enough' for you. Remember we have already defined the uses of money and how our success helps other people to succeed in their God-given purposes through our generosity. So, we keep on doing our best financially in order to help as many people as possible, starting with our own household, friends, strangers, widows and orphans.

Be consistent.

Focus on the Prize (The Big Game)

When you believe you have made it, it's easy to lose focus of the bigger prize. If we take time to develop an audacious life plan, the possibility is we will never achieve everything in our lifetime. This is how the generational mindset works. We are only stewards of what God has enabled us to have and produce in our lifetime, but our kids or additional heirs will have a better foundation to fulfil some of our dreams and then some more.

A story is told about David, the king, who had a grand plan to build a temple for God. But God knowing David's heart and contemplation sent to him a messenger who told him that as much as the temple was a great idea, it was neither to be built by him, nor in his lifetime. His son Solomon, who was to become king after him, was the one appointed to construct the temple for God. In the meantime, God instructed David to focus on building his own palace which would be his earthly reward for a great life of obedience to God.

And this is exactly what happened, David left the surface of the earth without fulfilling his wildest dream, but Solomon honored that dream and indeed built the temple for God.

What about our dreams? Are they big enough to transcend generations?

The financial discourse we are having in these pages is only one part of our life plan. We need to contend for a longer life agenda where we see our children and our children's children living a far much better life than ours. We need to work on a higher agenda that breaks past family limitations and ushers in a new family fabric and brand that prints our name on an eternal legacy of greatness, contribution, sacrifice, and true success.

People with this type of mentality cannot be easily distracted. No matter what deviations you throw at them they continue to run towards the prize that is set before them. There is no greater temporary satisfaction that is worth even their attention and time. Their lives are always occupied by the end game. We need to be in this class of possibility makers.

This is the only way we will sustain the course of financial freedom. If we get out of debt and build some financial security only to achieve personal success and enjoy life as long as it lasts, we will never really free our posterity from a beggary lifestyle. We need to contend for bigger things.

Avoid Excitement

I have a dear friend of mine, Motsamai, who usually admonishes me against 'excitement'. Every time I go shopping with this guy and I make some comments towards some 'shiny' thing he will say *"now you are getting excited"*. This form of excitement is the one that just inspires you to spend money on things you don't need. You spend just because you can.

This attitude can easily ruin your chances of sustaining the newly found financial independence. You don't simply go to the shopping mall because you need 'shopping therapy', as much as you may need to do this once in a while to remain human.

You avoid joining excited people on the bandwagon of a sales season and 'you get better deals there'. You know people have unique proclivities.

But as for you, your shopping or consumer agenda should always be driven by your newly formed principles. You need to hold on to the *functionality mentality* when planning or conducting your purchases; our new mantra becomes *'what do I need this thing for?'*.

The below inquiring snippets may help you sustain your sanity in shopping:

- Why do I need this thing?
- Do I have an existing alternative that I can use for the same purpose?

- What are the benefits of purchasing this item?
- Do I have a budget (allocated amount) for this item, or can I replace another budgeted item for this one?
- Can this thing wait until a certain month?
- Did I originally plan to buy this item or am I simply influenced by some good words from a friend, spouse, marketer, or salesperson?

One of the best spending advices says, it is always better to give yourself some thinking space before flashing the cash and buying that item on spot. I like taking a day or two to think about spontaneous purchases without the persuasion of 'losing a good deal'. I hope you know about the FOMO movement (the **F**ear **O**f **M**issing **O**ut). It can be a bad trap. Another one is YOLO (**Y**ou **O**nly **L**ive **O**nce). They both raise legitimate emotional inclinations towards living large and spending it all, but we need to apply our sober mental faculties before committing to any decision, even to non-financial decisions.

Another strange source of excitement is variable and non-structured income such as a bonus, commission, dividend, honorarium, trip allowances and the like. Cash from these sources is easy prey for unplanned expenditure. Somehow any unplanned cash drives our levels of adrenaline, and the financial side of the brain starts to get 'less than 20%' of restraint and discipline.

When you catch yourself getting excited and driving towards the shopping mall with no plan at all, just know that you are intoxicated with excitement. You may wish to make a U-Turn and drive towards home. Get a cup of tea or a nice shower and ponder about life.

You will realize that the cash excitement usually ebbs away if you simply ignore it.

Like Mindedness

Another important factor for sustaining your financial status is galvanizing your surroundings with like-minded people. You need to have your circle filled with people who think in wealth building patterns; who look forward to the future; who are excited about saving, keeping, and investing money like you; people who are never excited at the first instance of seeing or touching some silk or exotic fur coat.

Financial sanity requires tough skin as the world will continue to bombard you with opportunities to spend your hard-earned cash with the sole objective of taking you back to the trenches of debt.

I always consider personal financial management like going to the gym. You need to have a training buddy if you want to persist on the treadmill or that preferred elliptical machine. If you are like me, the first time I get to a new gym I am all excited and pumped up to try every piece of equipment. I will make sure to get into that gym every morning and ensure my body muscles appreciate the effort; or at least the mirrors should connive to deceive my eyes that I am building some muscle!

However, after a week or two, that excitement starts to wane-off. You are no longer as excited and pumped-up to go all the way. Sleep starts to elude you or personal projects just get in the way. Especially for writers like me, I always have to choose between finishing my book or a professional publication versus hitting the gym at 5:00AM.

The choice to prioritize the health-routine lies in the power of solid exercise and vitality partnerships. Apart from your well drafted health plan, you need a friend or that pestering neighbor to scream at you every morning and make sure you pick the training gear whilst shaking off sleep from your dozy eyes.

Same with finances. You need an accountability partner; it could be your spouse or your other good friend who doesn't shy away from screaming *'no Starbucks today!'*. Or would the scream sound better if it was *'no pizza tonight!'*? Better still, *'not another BMW buddy!'*

Do you know why these screams are important?

A fat bank account can be so intoxicating.

"Once beaten twice shy". We can't afford to return to the misery of being broke.

#don'tleaveyourmoneybehind

Becoming a Personal Finance Teacher

"Knowledge is only fulfilling when shared with others"

11

Chapter 11: Teaching Others

A worthy ancient saying goes, *"But the one who did not know and did what deserved punishment will receive a light beating. From everyone who has been given much, much will be required; and from the one who has been entrusted with much, even more will be expected."*

Personal learning and development alone is not sufficient. It is like getting all the billions of the world and hoarding them to your own destruction. *What would it profit a man?*

Whatever is shared grows. In other ways, it is given back to you in an equal measure. This is a trustworthy saying. Hence, if you truly desire far-reaching and generational impact, you must prepare your mind to generously share such knowledge with others. This is the only way to fully benefit from what you know and bring real satisfaction to your life.

I understand that there are cultures, ethnicities, territories, and personal DNAs that worship self-aggrandizement and selfishness. It should not be that way. We can't build nations in our own small spaces and individual efforts. It takes a whole generation to cause a major shift of national dynamics in economics, trade, history, culture, governance, and leadership. Whatever you know at expert level is worth sharing with your family, friends, generation, or to the succeeding generation. Do not embrace the custom of hoarding good things from people who need them.

This is the reason my 'forever teaching' rotates around giving, sharing, generosity, love, passion, growth, and national building. As a people, we need to learn that every blessing is like a baton, it must be passed on to the next person. Don't hide worthwhile and excellent information from others.

What I have learnt in my few years on this earth is that successful people *(i.e. people who got to the top through righteous and noble means)* don't usually hesitate to give or share their success secrets. They are, in fact, genuinely interested in the success of others; they love creating lots of 'mini-them' or at least students from their universities of hard-knocks). I believe most of such good people have a sense of making life doable for others; not in a destructive way by making other people lazy, but rather, it's as if they are saying *"why should others suffer like I did to get to the top?"*

For someone who has gone through the pain and the shame of receiving numerous telephone calls from the bank for loan default or interest delays, you wouldn't wish that kind of life for yourself or anyone, let alone your family and friends. That life can be humiliating and uncomfortable.

I remember an earlier experience of having a bank officer ask me if I could at least settle the minimum interest payment on my loan at a time when I couldn't even tell my right hand from the left hand. This was at a time when everything was a priority – food was crucial, transport was critical, kids' school fees was a must, utility bills were demanded like yesterday – and I could not breathe (literally). Explaining to the bank's customer services officer why I could not pay something as low as US$100 couldn't make sense. It neither made sense to me!

When you are working hard, and you are considered to be an honorable member of a society, people wouldn't expect you to have nothing in the bank account, especially when you are also seen to dress and drive well. No philosopher can explain this misfortune.

Hence, those of us who have walked this path of humiliation have a massive responsibility to share our experiences with others. It is up to them to learn, apply and avoid the common pitfalls of poor financial management, or at least for them to carve a wiser path towards their own financial freedom.

The following are some of the key considerations in this quest of teaching others and sharing our experiences:

Focus on the Friendship and Compassion

It is tough to convince others on any subject if you fail to create a bond of belonging, welfare, or friendship. It is easier to discuss personal finances with family, friends, and sometimes with colleagues. However, if your passion is to help as many people as possible on their financial freedom journey, it is important to see whether you are able to create better proximity before you thrust your ideas on them.

People are usually willing to listen to you when they can test your sincerity in the subject and your inclination towards their welfare or wellbeing.

It Is Never 'One Size Fits All'

Always remember that our life journeys are unique. Some people end up in financial mess due to, simply, bad choices. Not that they had any emergencies or disadvantage getting here; but rather they didn't know how to maximize their financial opportunities in their early career.

And there are some who sincerely got in a financial quagmire due to family emergencies, lost job opportunities, lack of educational funding, justifiable debt, among so many reasons.

We cannot make the mistake of just thinking every person ended up where they are because of carelessness or ignorance. If we truly desire to help people, we need to take time to hear their story and see how we can support each other morally, emotionally, physically, spiritually, and professionally. This is very important.

A deeper understanding of where people are coming from, and their current position also helps us to prescribe better 'financial medication'.

No case is a hopeless case. Everyone can be redeemed from the direst of financial messes.

Be Patient with People

Even your best friend can scream at you for trying hard to be a beneficial friend. These financial matters can be traumatic and depressing. I have known lots of people who gravitated from anxiety to depression because of financial problems. This story is not uncommon among expats across nations and continents.

Some of the anxiety emanates from the fact that people work hard every day just to pay back loans and survive. And this life is lived in a foreign land where your only hope is a work visa, temporary residency or indeed some form of government documentation that allows you passage to work in the land. It is not like your native home where you can pull strings of citizenship, family, and a deep friendship network. It just feels like you are alone on this journey of emancipation.

It's not a joke; financial problems in a foreign land can be depressing.

During the Covid19 pandemic season, many people lost jobs with no sufficient preparation time to sort out their bank loans first. For someone to lose the only reliable stream of income that was helping them to deal with the banks is draining, especially for expats living in countries which have no permanent resident visas or any chance for longer grace periods.

What would you do if the only way for you to save your family from a financial debacle is to sell all you have, including assets or investments in your home country, or face the arm of the law? So, when we are talking to people (especially after our own emancipation), appreciate that others are still fighting their battles to get to where we are.

Understand their pain and appreciate their 'hustle'.

More Encouragement Than Force

What people need in a time of financial stress is encouragement and spiritual support, reassuring them that they will be alright, and God will not abandon them. Our motivation needs to be sincere and based on a faithful foundation.

People are willing to listen, learn, and adapt quickly if they see that we are motivating them for their own good, and that we don't have a foreign agenda to force them into something they are not able or willing to do. Ultimately, always remember it's their life and not ours.

Be practical in your encouragement by offering your life journey and practical examples. If other people also helped you towards your financial freedom, talk about such people and how their support helped to unleash the shackles of debt from your feet.

Continue to Sharpen Your Own Saw

As stated by Stephen Covey, *"Your economic security does not lie in your job; it lies in your own power to produce—to think, to learn, to create, to adapt. That's true financial independence. It's not having wealth; it's having the power to produce wealth."* As we teach and encourage others, it is paramount that we also continue to sharpen our own saw to ensure we move from simply having money to creating enduring wealth, life experiences, and impact.

Sustainable wealth creation is the only way that guarantees eternal financial freedom and more time to impact the multitudes. It also assures us of generational wealth transfer to our children and our children's children.

We can continue learning about wealth creation through engagements with investment and wealth advisors, seminars, investment forums, relevant quality friends, and so many avenues. Simply, we need to be intentional about continuous personal development and living impactful lives.

There are so many ways we can contribute to the masses as well. As discussed earlier, one of our core missions can be to support widows and orphans, religious bodies, educational or professional institutes, and many other philanthropic organizations. You only need to choose a financial support path that aligns with your life principles, standards, and beliefs. Whichever path you choose, *it is always better to give than to receive.*

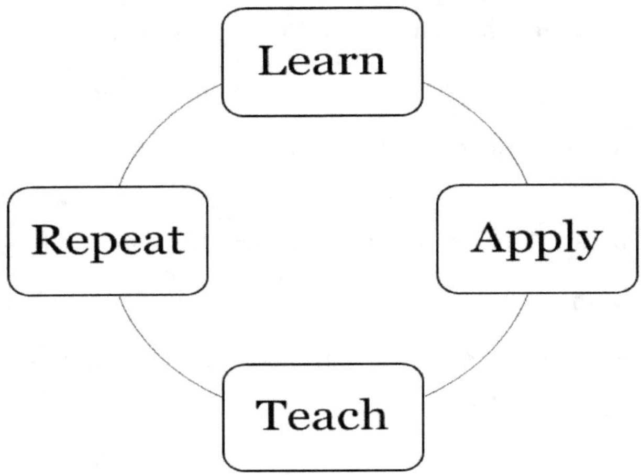

Once we have learned through our experiences and failures, be generous with the knowledge by sharing it with others.

#don'tleaveyourmoneybehind

With good focus, tenacity, and intentionality, the expat journey can be both enjoyable and fulfilling.

#don'tleaveyourmoneybehind

ABOUT THE AUTHOR

Moses Chavi is a believer in change and progress. He is an acclaimed Malawian writer, speaker, and coach. He is a Fellow of the Association of Certified Chartered Accountants-UK, Certified Internal Auditor and Certified Risk Manager under the Institute of Internal Auditors (USA); a Certified Fraud Examiner (ACFE-USA); and Certified Manager from The Institute of Certified Professional Managers.

Moses is a corporate governance expert, an entrepreneur, and a leadership advocate, and has worked as a consultant with Deloitte and KPMG, two of the global Big 4 auditing and consulting firms, and has audited and advised multi-national corporations, public entities, investment firms, and family businesses in Africa and the Middle East, gaining experience living in 7 countries.

As of 2023, Moses has contributed more than 150 professional articles to professional magazines and a Malawian business newspaper, and his professional insights were covered in the feature publications of the Internal Auditor Magazine and ACCA's Global AB Magazine in 2020 and 2022, respectively. He has facilitated various professional training courses for audit and risk practitioners and business leaders.

Email: moschavi@gmail.com

LinkedIn: https://www.linkedin.com/in/moseschavi/

Twitter: @Moschavi

Facebook: Facebook.com/moschavi

www.ingramcontent.com/pod-product-compliance
Lightning Source LLC
LaVergne TN
LVHW052254200926
848481LV00002B/364
9798889553847